The Caravaggio Bible

Mario Dal Bello

The Caravaggio Bible

Images from the Old and New Testament

SCHNELL + STEINER

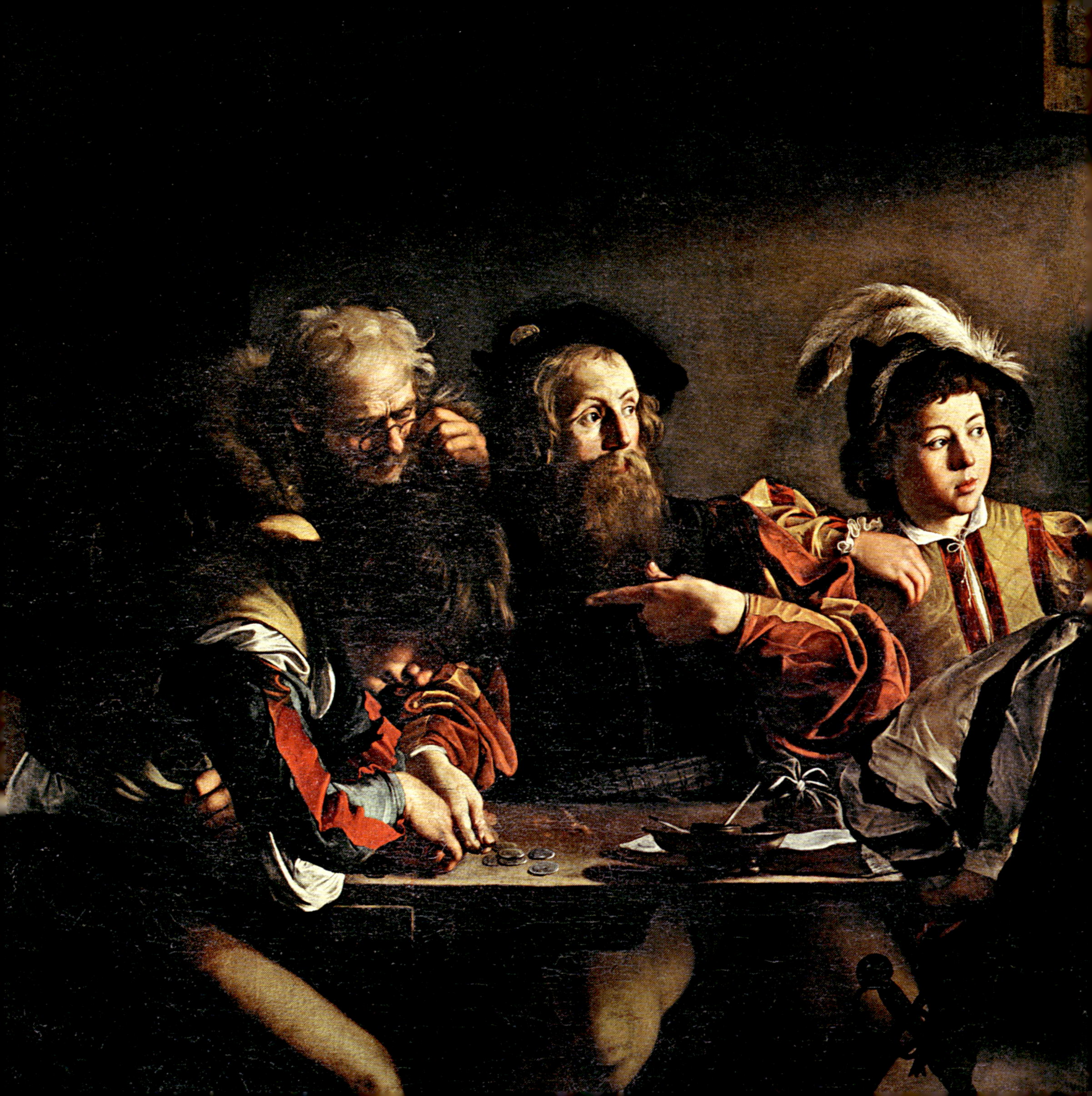

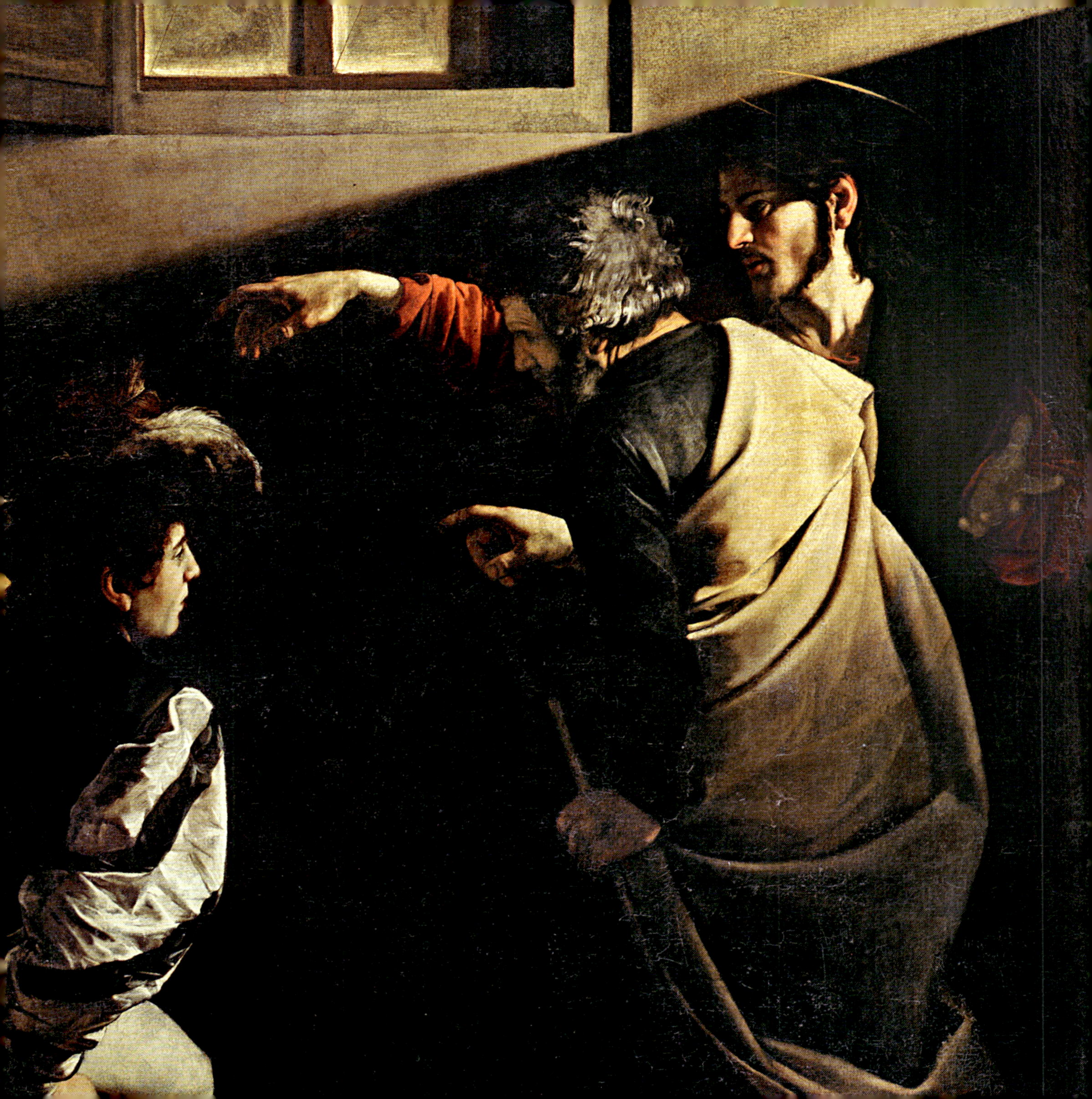

Front cover: Michelangelo Merisi da Caravaggio: The Calling of
Saint Matthew (Rome, San Luigi dei Francesi, Photography:
Stefano Fabi)

Image credits:
p .4/5, 14, 52: Stefano Fabi
p. 24, 30, 38, 46, 56, 62, 68, 70, 74, 80, 82: bpk/Scala
p. 28: akg-images/Erich Lessing
p. 34: Nancy, Musée des Beaux-Arts/Angelo Lubino
p. 40, 44, 50: akg-images/Electa
p. 58, 64: akg-images
p. 76: bpk – Stiftung Preußische Schlösser und Gärten Berlin-
Brandenburg/Gerhard Murza
p. 86: bpk/RMN/Paris, Musée du Louvre/René-Gabriel Ojéda

Cover design: Anna Braungart, Tübingen
Image processing and layout: Florian Knörl, Erhardi Druck GmbH
Print: Erhardi Druck GmbH, Regensburg
Translation: Dr. Manjula Dias-Hargarter

Bibliographic information published by the Deutsche Nationalbibliothek
The Deutsche Nationalbibliothek lists this publication in the Deutsche
Nationalbibliografie; detailed bibliographic data are available in the
Internet at http://dnb.d-nb.de.

First edition 2010
© 2010 Verlag Schnell & Steiner GmbH,
Leibnizstr. 13, D-93055 Regensburg
ISBN 978-3-7954-2370-4

Further information about our publications can be found under:
www.schnell-und-steiner.de

Content

Preface

"Art is meant to disturb; science reassures" (L'art est fait pour troubler; la science rassure). This declaration by the French Cubist and friend of Picasso, George Braque, provides us with a motto of sorts that consolidates the collective response to Caravaggio's work. Indeed, his paintings contain an extraordinary tension, are powerfully charged with emotion, and to this end, are meant to cause marvel and consternation. They reflect an outright brilliance, but also a brief, tortured existence, similar to a meteor, that nonetheless casts its light into the following centuries, specifically, not so much through the spiritual emulation of the so-called Caravaggesques but rather by the expressive power of his own creations.

Light is undoubtedly the most effective medium used by the artist in order to "disturb" the conscience. It assumes a special significance in Caravaggio's 21 paintings with religious subjects that constitute the thematic focus of the following volume. His splendid beams of light make their way through the darkness of scenes from the Gospel, almost appearing as rays of divine mercy within the somber stories of mankind. One imagines, for example, the shallow light which enters from the side window in *The Calling of Saint Matthew*: it rests upon the two main figures and emphasizes in particular, the extended index finger of Christ (a quotation from Michelangelo's *Creation of Adam* in the Sistine Chapel), whereby the calling to a new creation becomes a transformation of the tax collector Levi into the apostle Matthew.

Caravaggio accomplishes a type of artistic exegesis of the Holy Scripture, whereas he mainly focuses upon Christ and the stories of the Gospel. However, in addition to the obvious counterpoint between light and shadow, or grace and sin, an additional line of interpretation exists: namely, the central theme of incarnation. The portrayed scenes and faces belong to everyday life; they are not highly stylized into transcendent icons, but instead reflect the work and daily routine of the people; that is, they carry the entire burden of historical experience upon themselves. Christ himself is depicted in an almost extreme corporeality, which – as in the *Incredulity of Saint Thomas* in Potsdam – by the apostle's finger that probes the wound in Christ's side, can be touched and explored in a fully realistic manner.

In the "gallery" of Caravaggio's religiously-inspired paintings, the message of the Evangelist "and the Word was made flesh" (John 1:14) finds various forms of expression, which also means that the faithful are offered various possibilities to hear the word of life (compare 1 John 1:1), to see it with their own eyes, to gaze upon it, and to grasp it in their hands. In this manner, we are led to the heart of the Christian message, and the master from Lombardy becomes – in his way – its witness and annunciator. The prominent position of his Passion scenes, which display an inconceivable pain (the typical symbol of humanity), clearly proves this: God of the Gospel is no stoic ruler, he does not live reclusively in the golden heavens of transcendence, but stands shoulder to shoulder with the suffering human race. Through the reflection of divine light, his stations of the cross become the paschal way of light: from the *via crucis* to the *via lucis*.

In the following pages, Mario Dal Bello serves as the qualified, irreplaceable guide into the heart of the unique sequence of sacred images by Michelangelo Merisi. His discerning inquiries, devoid of academicism, reveal before our eyes the "painted word," not only in terms of its most elevated beauty, but also in its truth, which captivated the faithful as well as the religiously indifferent.

The Italian poet Umberto Saba wrote in the mid-20th century: "Every work of art is a confession." Caravaggio's painting is simply a revelation of intimate spirituality and personality. However, it also becomes an invocation to the viewer, to shake himself from his quest and his inner turmoil, his inner tension and his religious agitation.

Gianfranco Ravasi
President of the Pontifical Council for Culture and of
the Pontificial Commission for the Cultural Heritage
of the Church

Preface

For many years, I have thoroughly considered the issue of faith of the major Christian artists from the period between the Quattrocento and the second half of the 17th century. Based upon a series of erroneous assumptions, many have dismissed the years in question as not entirely Christian, in fact, as anti-Christian. Within the collective imagination (and indebted to a historicist ideology), contradictory and wholly false images emerged of a dark, backward, quasi-primitive Middle Age, which nonetheless shone through its artists, and of a cultured, sophisticated Renaissance, which was nonetheless the expression of a worldly, if not proto-laicistic world view. In this context, Leonardo da Vinci was frequently regarded as anti-Catholic, even as a model of an anarchist *ante litteram*, who blindly followed scientific principles and abandoned every religious world view in favor of a dependence upon science and technology. Michelangelo emerged as an intellectual, who in the tangle of questions regarding mankind, espoused Protestantism. Finally, Caravaggio, who was not stripped of his extraordinary, innate adaptability, would become an individual solely driven by instinct, partial to every sacrilege and vice. These stereotypes are the fruit of art historical research that is bound to the respective spirit of the age and led by ideals or even ideologies. Yet due to their importunity, they have become entrenched in some areas and are difficult to remedy.

One such type of art history is often based upon good intentions as well as poor practice of the discipline regarding methodological inadequacies and lack of knowledge (or ignorance) of the historical as well as art historical circumstances. Moreover, art and the history of art are certainly not immune to false assumptions, so that errors sometimes emerge from prefabricated opinions, which systematically distort the facts. In order to honor the truth: in the last century, art historical research has yielded significant developments. For example – using Marco Calvesi's research as a point of departure – attempts have been made to wash away the thick grimy layer of demonization which has increasingly obfuscated Caravaggio over the years.

Twenty years of serious research disproved once and for all his image as a anti-Christian artist. Earnest and likewise broad-minded studies with an interdisciplinary approach have led to an understanding of the theological content of Leonardo da Vinci's works; even the mystical dimensions of Michelangelo's art was honored, which not least of all is indebted to the poetry of the *Roman Triptych* penned by by Pope John Paul II. The consequences of the ideologized writing of history, which dominated the academic scene between the 1940s and 1950s, are nonetheless still noticeable, and not only in the area of theory, but – perhaps even more so – in the actual artistic realm.

Certain terms appear to be displaced by misconceptions and unclear definitions in such a way that their meaning must be unraveled with the utmost care. In this way, for example, there existed a multitude of meanings for the terms "style" and "art" - which were contradictory up until now. "Style" is not a synonym for "art," for it consistently involves a partial quantity, a method, of classifying all principles of art according to a nuance and a particular quality. In doing so, style cannot ever – as unique as it may be – completely question the principles and basis of art, otherwise it would not, by definition, involve a style of art. It would approach the foundation of something new, which although perhaps interesting, is not "art," for it would not correspond to its constitutive basic principles. Since the beginning, art has involved beauty above all else; beauty is the model and purpose of art. Were that no longer true, we would stand in front of a work of man that we could no longer call "art" and that would no longer belong to the scope of the "fine arts." In our time, we have sought out – on the foundation of what seems to me a rather confusing definition of art - precedents of the modern, current, rebelliousness or nihilism in the past. This creates confusion not only among art enthusiasts, but also among its patrons and even its "artists." There is a true notion of contemporaneity, which is always valid in art, and it has always been applied to Christian art, in order to express in each case the message of the Gospel in a contemporary manner and within the framework of the golden rule of art. We can see this, for example, in *The Calling of Saint Matthew*: the contemporary figure (in the form of a tax-collector and in Matthew himself) is portrayed in his actual encounter with Christ. The clothing and behavior of the depicted figures were so familiar to the people of the late 16th century that they were immediately able to identify the protagonist of the tale from the Gospel of Matthew.

Mario Dal Bello has plumbed Caravaggio's art in many directions and in great depth, especially with regard to the clear intentions of the artist, to depict the mystery of incarnation through the tremendously expressive power of art. Thus the title of the volume is not a pretense; it truly reveals a far-reaching aspect of this extraordinary artistic personality, who despite all the troubles of everyday life, was able to explain the beauty of his belief and what is more, several centuries later, shows us the way to true art.

Rodolfo Papa
Art Historian, Artist
Lecturer at the Pontifical
Urbaniana University – Rome

Introduction

To write a book at the present about Michelangelo Merisi da Caravaggio, better known as Caravaggio, entails risk. For one, the literature about the painter is already so vast and moreover, ever-expanding, that an additional text about him may appear superfluous. Secondly, the proposed theme of "The Caravaggio Bible" does not consider a specific pictorial cycle, as is the case with – to name a few famous examples – Michelangelo's frescoes for the Sistine Chapel, those by Raphael and his assistants for the Vatican loggia (the so-called "Raphael Bible"), or Tintoretto's paintings in Venice for the Scuola Grande di San Rocco. However, when Caravaggio's entire *oeuvre* is taken into account, his apparently strong preference for Biblical subjects, as well as his detailed, continuous preoccupation with a number of major themes from the Old and New Testaments, justify the title of this volume. This is strengthened by the fact that Caravaggio's approach and interpretation are absolutely unmatched and display a strong personal sympathy, so that all of his works with religious content can be considered as a single entity. Moreover, his point of view is distinctly "Christ-centered" and in fact, appropriate to its era – a point which shall be addressed later – yet at the same time, strongly autobiographical.

With Caravaggio, the outlook on life and image of man are unique and fundamentally dramatic, as the Biblical message often is. It is increasingly filled with the entire personality of the artist, more so due to an inner need and his often painful life experiences, versus being based upon an intellectual concept. In this way, the message is direct and clear.

Thus, the Caravaggio Bible becomes the artistically-infused "painted word." It emphasizes a number of specific aspects of the texts, constructs them in stages of a visual commentary on the history of salvation, and makes them relevant to daily life.

To this day, all of this makes Caravaggio's work so fascinating and so different from his contemporaries, justifying the research for the current text. In the present volume, the works of art will be analyzed using individual descriptions and occasionally, in comparison to other versions of the same subject. One can repeatedly view Caravaggio's paintings and discover a new detail within them every time, which tellingly demonstrates how astutely the painter was able to penetrate the Biblical text, make it his own, and then, infused with a personal touch, offer it to the observers and the faithful.

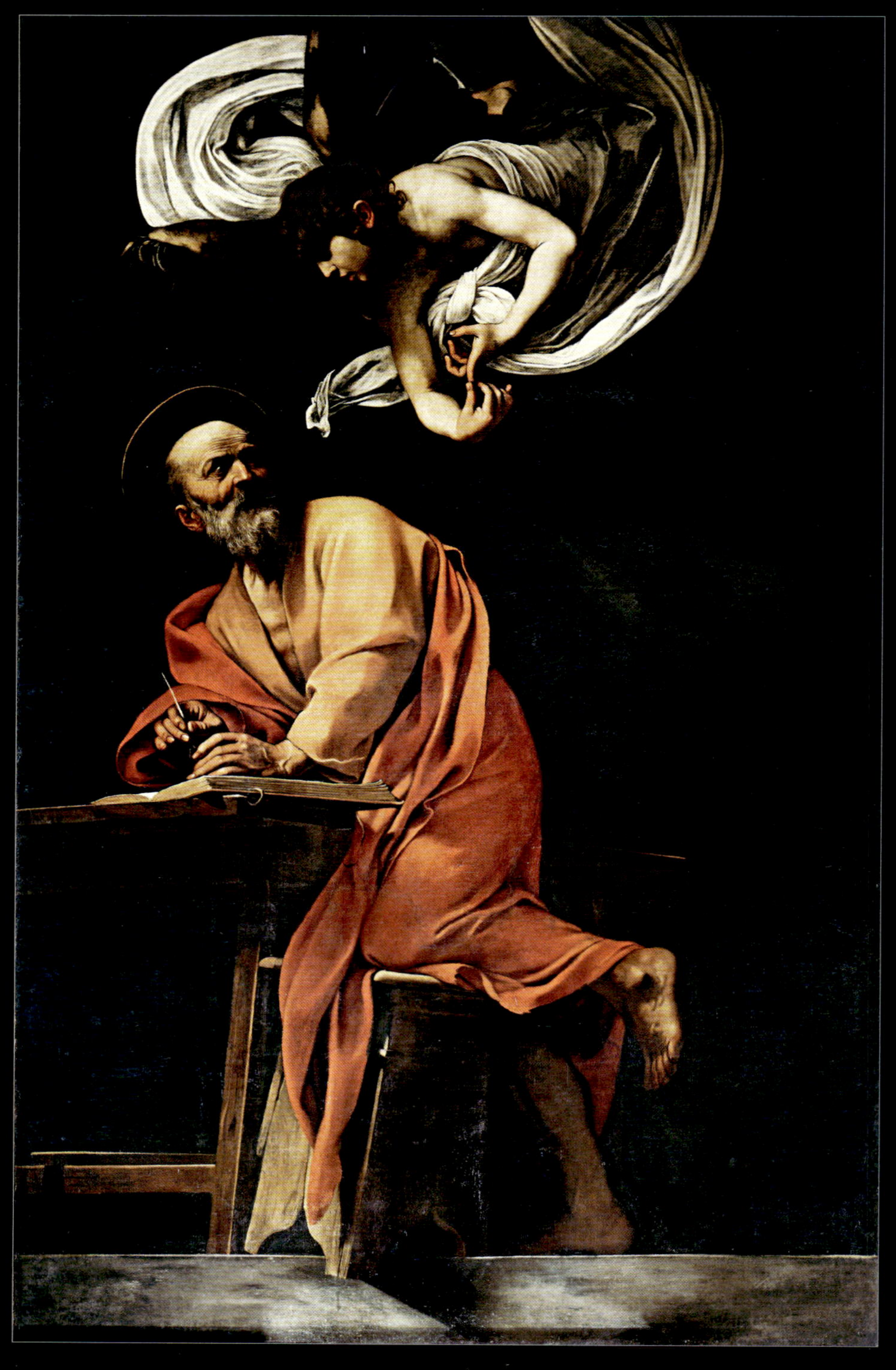

Sacred Art in Rome During the Counter-Reformation: From the Late Works of Michelangelo to the Carracci Family

The decrees of the Council of Trent brought a clear turning point to the Catholic Church with regard to religious images. On the one hand, one wished to strengthen the function of sacred art as the *biblia pauperum* ("Pauper's Bible," which religious paintings had in fact been for centuries) via the avowed return to simplicity and dignity, but also through a direct understanding of depicted themes. Conversely, one wanted to react to the meager spiritual depth of a number of religious works from previous years, while those which re-appropriated Classicism were often regarded as a new heathenism.

The trauma of Protestant rebellion and the resulting split of Europe prompted the Catholic Church – especially individuals such as Pope Paul IV Carafa and Saint Charles Borromeo, Archbishop of Milan – to decisively exert their influence on artistic decisions. It is no coincidence that Paul IV, in particular, considered having Michelangelo's *Last Judgment* torn down because it appeared "obscene" to him. Other popes, from Gregory XIII to Sixtus V, had campaigned for the rediscovery of the "sacred Rome" of the catacombs and martyrs, while a majority of mostly Lombard and Flemish artists developed a celebratory and piety-oriented pictorial language.

The rise of new orders – such as the Capuchins, who revived Franciscan spirituality, the Jesuits with their support of culture, the various brotherhoods who supported and tended to the ill, and the Oratorians of the Florentine Philipp Neri, who through art, theater, and music, gained distinction in the educational system – also led to a simplified representation of sacred stories. They were intended to be easily understood by and accessible to the faithful. The goal was to return to the purity of ancient Christianity.

The late work of Michelangelo (from the 1540s onward), as well as the Vatican's Pauline Chapel and his sketches and sculptures conveyed a tense and emotional religious sentiment. After Michelangelo's death (1564), artists of religious images devoted themselves to his expressively powerful style, as well as to Raphael's gracefulness: images emerged that were clearly "catachetical" and with a distinct theatrical, pathetic, and spiritual character. The cycle of the Passion of Christ and other stories from the Gospel significantly increased, on the one hand, in order to confirm the role of the Catholic Church as the single guard of truth, and on the other hand, in order to soothe, to urge the faithful to attend to their spiritual life. Up until the pontificate of Clement VIII, who celebrated the Holy Year in 1600 with great ceremoniousness, a broad offensive of the Catholic Church against Protestantism and the new evangelization of the populace permeated many new works of art, especially in the areas of painting and sculpture, so as to portray Catholicism and the papal attempts at reform in a favorable light. Art became once again the tool of propaganda and catechesis.

Thus emerged a style whose precedents were Michelangelo, Raphael, and Correggio, and which were capable of integrating power with empathy in representations of the Gospel. Especially popular were illustrations of suffering and the resurrection of Jesus. Of those in which the Crucifixion always serves as the focal point, the most significant is the one in the Oratorio del Gonfalone, completed in Rome (1570–1575) with its twelve stories of Christ by various Late Mannerists, including Marco Pino and Federico Zuccari. Each painting is dominated by a Messiah who stands above the event, glorious even in suffering; he appears serene within a classical setting where various figures act with forced, theatrical poses. The constant reference to the highly-esteemed Raphael and Michelangelo becomes especially clear in the *Resurrection* by Marco Pino.

A significant artist on account of his individual style and his influence throughout Italy is Federigo Barocci. He came from Urbino, but was also active in Rome, especially in the Chiesa della Vallicella, the locus of activity and burial place of Saint Philipp Neri. Barocci is an educated, intelligent painter, who integrated the teachings of the Old Masters into a new, unique language of forms. In his scenes, emotionalism is kept under control; theatricality is balanced. He applies luminous pigments and soft light. His paintings express feelings of great magnitude, yet are never exaggerated. The figures are, without exception, dressed in ancient clothing, while their environment is often domestic, with animals, flowers, and fruits. Idyllic moments (such as the *Rest on the Flight to Egypt* – Rome, Vatican) alternate with dramatic ones (*Descent From the Cross* – Perugia Cathedral). Many of his contemporaries view Barocci as a model of art that is convincing without being coarse.

Along the same lines but with greater expressive strength was Annibale Carracci from Bologna. Like numerous contemporaries, including Guido Reni, Guercino, and Domenichino, he moved to Rome at the beginning of the 17th century. There, he devised a greatly noble, classical style, as seen in both in his mythological frescoes (Rome, Palazzo Farnese) as well as his Biblical scenes (*Lamentation of Christ* – Naples, Museum Capodimonte). The paths of these artists shall clash with that of Caravaggio's, adopting his style to an extent while departing from it in other ways. In taking on religious and especially Christological subjects, however, they shall never achieve the passionate emotion of a Michelangelo Merisi. Despite all of their naturalistic details, their art remains a lofty and noble one, thus greatly distanced from Caravaggio's wild vitality, which goes on to create utter scandal for the art world.

This is the artistic and cultural milieu in which the Lombard painter is active after his move from Milan to Rome: an "academic" art, obligated to the standards of the former great masters, interwoven with the need for a direct, simplified method of communication and a deeper, more graceful religiosity.

The Main Characteristics of Caravaggio's Sacred Art

For Caravaggio, like his artistic contemporaries, there exists a predominance of commissions with religious subjects. In particular, they involve the life of Christ and specific stories from the Old Testament that were very popular at the time, such as *The Sacrifice of Isaac* or *Judith and Holofernes*. However, Caravaggio's interpretation is completely new. Of course, he was influenced by his Lombard-Venetian training, which tended towards realism and the emphasis of color as a chief component, as well as his contacts to Classicism and his masters in Rome, as well as specific elements of Middle European art. However, what interests Caravaggio most of all is man. His search for an artistic means of expression moves entirely in this direction, so that everything that involves human existence, in all its feelings, emotions, and tensions, become a focal point of his works. The depth of his psychological penetration, his search for inner being, his personal involvement in what is depicted, created astonishment and scandal in his time, not least of all owing to the unleashed power with which he approached his work. Indeed, potency combined with authenticity is the hallmark of Caravaggio's art and his method of representing Biblical events. It only stands to reason that because of it, he encountered disconcertment and even protest, for he was clearly opposed to the placid, assuring Biblical images of his contemporaries.

However, Caravaggio was aligned with the demands of the Counter-Reformation with its "pauperism of the Gospel" preached by Philipp Neri and Charles Borromeo, with its concern to the underprivileged, but above all, with a reading of the Gospel, which could be genuinely experienced on a daily basis. His "realism" or "naturalism," however one chooses to call it, results not only from his Lombard origins, but from a need to relay the Gospel narratives in such a way that is embedded not in the past, but in the present. This also means that they could and should reoccur in this present, hence his preference for the simple folk, shown in their usual activities, within their typical environment, and with authentic facial expressions. What emerges and resonates is a dimension of truth, for the holy scenes are close to the people and thus authentic.

Caravaggio's art becomes highly eloquent, not because it would be rhetorical or elaborate, but in the sense that it speaks to the viewer. His painting is always "speaking" – thus, the "painted Word," and Christ truly becomes the God "who has become man." He is a man like us and is therefore often seized with deeply human feelings such as pain, surprise, defeat, or confidence. However, this man who becomes God never abandons his actual purpose. Even under highly dramatic circumstances, he remains the Messiah who endures everything, but holds steadfast in his decision.

Above all, Caravaggio solidifies Christ's inner strength in his facial expressions. The faces of Christ are captivatingly beautiful: they have nothing of the beauty of Raphael's or Michelangelo's paintings, they are not idealized, they possess common, sometimes portrait-like features. Yet the painter invests them with his unique light, so that despite their coarse physiognomy – such as in *The Incredulity of Thomas* – they retain a clearly spiritual grace.

Caravaggio's Christ is equivalent to the three synoptic Evangelists (Marc, Matthew, and Luke), in that his humanity is accentuated: exhaustion, anger, tenderness, decisiveness, exertion, pain, outcry. Thus, he is wholly human, capable of identifying with every man and vice versa.

However, the component of mystery always remains. Caravaggio investigates this aspect with an often poignant empathy. The Jesus who is lost in thought with the young men from Emmaus (Milan) or the composed figure of the *Ecce Homo* in Genoa, each one surrounded in light as well as shadow, testify to the barely fathomable essence of an experience far beyond our reach. Caravaggio may pause at every arcane threshold leading to the subjectivity of consciousness; this threshold escapes us, but he does not forsake it so as to comprehend it. Because of this, he does not escape from the dramatic events of the Easter Triduum. The entire Passion is explored and newly interpreted. For some scenes, two different versions are made, with acute spiritual perspicacity and extraordinary expressiveness, for it is the Passion of every man, and his own, that of the artist. The scenes of the Flagellation, the Crowning of Thorns, as well as the Supper in Emmaus display a naturally-ordered contrast between violence and amazement. Its deep inner potency calls forth an immediately emotional sympathy. The depicted figure captures us, it never leaves us indifferent, for one senses that the the artist was the first one to be affected.

It is also possible to speak of a "Christology of Caravaggio." Within it, the stately theme of the Pietà, namely, the loving contemplation of the Passion of Jesus that was especially popular during the Middle Ages, becomes interpreted as a modern, contemporary drama of man in his inseparable unity between soul and body, that is wholly and truthfully expressed. In this regard, Caravaggio approaches Shakespeare.

The painter demonstrates the same analytical abilities with regard to images of other saints. Magdalene and Mary are most frequent. As was typical of the period, women from the general population served as his models, who were sketched in his studio and then newly interpreted upon the canvas. His realism is a description of things and people, but not as they appear in reality, rather, how he interprets them, for he possesses the ability not to describe what is true, but instead, "to invent what is true" and to make it universal and valid over time.

The Magdalenes and Marys are young and not-so-young women with full faces, large eyes, controlled contours: their gaze (as in the *Madonna di Loreto* in Rome or in *The Seven Works of Mercy* in Naples) is full of tenderness, but they also know decisiveness (as in *Judith*) or pensive calm (*Flight to Egypt* or *Birth of Christ*). In every instance, they involve strong personalities that display no weakness. Caravaggio understands the very feminine capability of tenacious, courageous love.

In all of his works, in what might be called a "dramatic theater" of humanity, the painter depicts every human type and character. Thus, John the Baptist is a study of youth, the apostles project an outlook of maturity and age. It is the life of man, in its various phases and experiences, which is captured and illustrated by Caravaggio through the Biblical narratives that show the divine presence within history.

His art is anchored in the present, in the here and now. Caravaggio does not paint for eternity in the manner of Michelangelo, who for example, devised for his *Conversion of Saint Paul* (Vatican, Pauline Chapel) a large, crowded scene with surreal colors and sculp-turally formed bodies, therefore choosing a place beyond space and time. For the same subject in Santa Maria del Popolo (Rome), Caravaggio chose an enclosed, narrow room for a saint whose conversion takes place in a purely internal sense. Here, there is no Christ who blinds Paul, as in the case of Michelangelo, and in the picture there is only a stable boy and a horse. The story takes place here and now; God intervenes in the present.

Light is therefore revealed little by little; it is not crystal clear like Buonarroti, but emanates from the shadows, often bisecting the canvas and emphasizing the truthfulness of the experience. The "Caravag-gesque light" thus has a tangible as well as moral significance: it is God's mercy, which – like a wedge – finds its way to Matthew's calling; it is the familiarity and warmth of Christ's birth; it is the painful strength in the body of the flagellated Christ. And it comes – as typical with the Lombard painters – out of darkness. The shadow is therefore not a simple physi-cal darkness, but an equally spiritual night, a spiritual drama, as in the last version of *David and Goliath*, in which the giant emerges from the dark background into the light. With Caravaggio, shadow always creates life.

Life itself is represented by the "speaking" bodies. The figures Caravaggio illustrates are not beautiful in the traditional sense of the word; they are not idealized. Their harmony is of a vastly different type as that of the contemporaries Carracci, Reni, or Cesari, who upheld traditional standards, for Caravaggio's are based upon the unity between body and soul. With him, each individual's inner experience is expressed through the body. The lonely ascetic of a Saint Jerome is articulated, depending upon the situation, in turbulent or meditative old men; their weary bodies speak of an "ugly" beauty, which is not anti-classical, but extro-classical. Furrowed brows, like the crucified Peter in Santa Maria del Popolo, contain a expressive-ness which propels a new form of beauty: not that of the idealized, but of what is experienced. Furthermore, for Caravaggio, life is always worth living. It is no coincidence that in one of his last paintings, he presents himself twice: once in the youthful, pale, perfect oval face of David and then in the stony countenance of Goliath, a manifestation of his own fear of death. These forms of beauty are not opposing; they are complementary, for the painter speaks of two diverging excerpts from the same life.

 And so, we arrive at the discussion of the strongly biographical components of Caravaggio's "divine" images. There is almost nothing in which he has not depicted himself, sometimes even twice, as in the aforementioned *David and Goliath* or in the *Resurrec-tion of Lazarus* (Messina) which we shall investigate later. However, it never refers to a simple self-portrait, as a quasi-signature or extra, as seen in many of Titian's paintings, for instance. In the exact same way that his contemporary Dürer dared to paint a portrait of himself as the young Christ, Caravaggio fully immersed himself into the narrative. In doing so, he wishes to say that the experiences portrayed affect him deeply, for they occur not in the past, but in the here and now.

It appears at times as if the artist wanted to take a personal, spiritually-motivated journey in order to eventually reach an "illuminated path." Upon examining his biography, one can imagine a longed-for papal reprieve (that is, a more peaceful existence) after years of suffering and escape.

Caravaggio's realism is therefore a sum of particular qualities. First of all, because – as it is widely known – he painted with models in his workshop, and these contrived stagings impart his paintings with a clearly theatrical component. Caravaggio used the bodies of his actress-models in the manner of a director, calculating their poses and body language and establishing them either in their entirety, as half-figures, or as closeups, according to the dramatic effect he wished to achieve. In this way, the seemingly spontaneous gestures of his characters are, in fact, always the result of utmost observation and direction, in order to – as it has already been said – to invent what is true.

His realism is consistently thought out to the last detail. We could define it as a "realism of the soul," that is, of being human in every aspect, a special "interpretation" of definitive moments of human history via the Gospel narratives. These become a type of mirror to the history of man, which is rediscovered within them. In turn, Christ reflects the story of humankind through his existence: that is, Biblical stories and the history of man coincide.

In this regard, the development of the artist is by no means linear; vacillations and contradictions exist. One must only think about the differing versions of the same subject (*Conversion on the Way to Damascus, Supper at Emmaus, David and Goliath…*). Particularly decisive is his use of light and color.

We have already mentioned the dramatic, vital function of light and shadow. Towards the end of his life, the painter seems to have place an increasingly greater emphasis upon shadow. Light becomes weaker, occasionally appearing only as small flashes of light (i.e., *Martyrdom of Saint Ursula*, Naples), the so-called "words of the soul." Moreover, color, which in earlier paintings was still luminous, pastose, and soft, becomes over time almost narrowed, or more accurately, based upon fewer basic pigments: red, white, black. These are applied in variations that are both beautiful and often infused with pain and presented almost as "voices" of people or of the scene being portrayed. The highest level of this is found in the neutral backgrounds of the Maltese and Sicilian works, which Caravaggio conceived with a decisive moral goal and an unprecedented psychological intensity.

These works are – typical of the painter – multivoiced and expansively arranged, even when only one or two figures are seen upon the canvas. With Caravaggio, a general, universally relevant aspect is always evident, which is expressed in a dynamic, at times aggressive, but never constant manner.

Merisi's art is consistently "happening" and never an adulation of a past event. Moreover, despite his reputation as a "lapsed" Catholic, his deep religiosity enabled him to penetrate the deepest levels of the narrative with an uncanny sincerity.

The "Caravaggio Bible" thus becomes a painted observation of the path of human history, by a God-man who leads the earthly inhabitants from the darkness into light, from pain towards hope. In fact, hope is the dimension which underlies the entire sacred history as told by Caravaggio and develops therein an expressive power beyond the everyday. This power was once a cause of scandal and of a fascination that we still sense now. It is a characteristic of a Caravaggesque creation of art. And this – not only artistic – strength is passed on to other artists, Rembrandt among others. However, he does not limit himself, as simple imitators did, to the special effects of chiaroscuro or a superficial realism, but rather, he grasped the unique moral and spiritual depths of the Christian framework that was Caravaggio's.

Stories From the Old Testament

Of the Old Testament subjects that have been frequently depicted in the visual arts, Caravaggio has painted only three: The Sacrifice of Isaac, Judith and Holofernes, and David and Goliath. The angle from which Caravaggio regards these figures is that of a keen investigation of intensely dramatic moments, examined with psychological finesse, paired with the most gruesome aspects of human atrocity.

Earlier examples – from the Lombard to the Tuscan to the Roman painters – belong to the cultural property of the artist, who in one fell swoop, abandoned past representations and even those of his contemporaries, opting to create a "theater of human souls" in its most violent and/or most subtle expressions. In this manner, the religious subject is explored with a depth and wealth of significance that was completely new for the audience of that period.

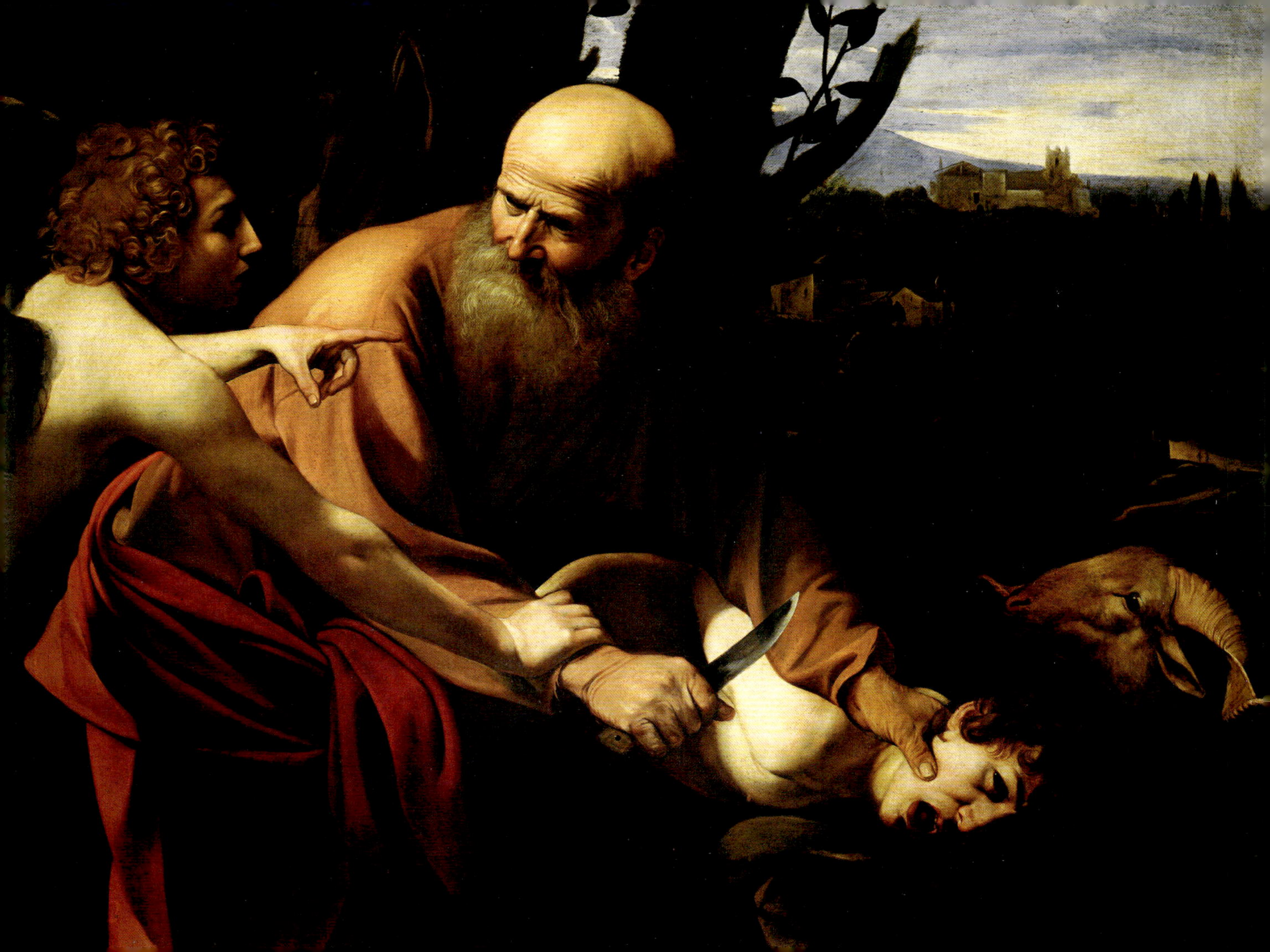

1. The Sacrifice of Isaac

Oil on canvas, 104 x 135 cm. Florence, Uffizi.

The story from the 22nd chapter of the Book of Genesis was usually depicted with a strong emphasis upon the dramatic. Caravaggio created this version in 1603 for Maffeo Barberini, an educated prelate, whose portrait he would also paint and who would later become Pope Urban VIII.
The emotional scene is played out in front of one of Caravaggio's very rare landscapes; he had long since freed himself from the Venetian style of painting, cultivating a sensibility that defied categorization and even appears to have anticipated some Impressionists. Light strikes the body of the angel from the left; from there, it radiates upon Isaac, who screams beneath the threatening knife in his father's hand. It is the centerpiece of the story. The angel points with his finger at the ram at the right edge of the painting. Leonardo had invented this gesture, which was later adopted by many painters in order to indicate divine intervention. Abraham is one of the bareheaded, beaded strong old men, invented by Tintoretto, frequently painted by Caravaggio, and a standard of the Baroque Period. The gestural potency of the angel – with his classic, even boyish contours – is sustained by the light that nearly bisects the canvas and is revealed in his hands: the one hand points, the other grasps Abraham's wrist.

Through the angel, God manifests his power to the figure of Abraham. He is illuminated by the angel's light, which also draws out the contours of the trees from the darkness (possibly recalling Giorgione's *Three Philosophers*) to then rapidly move towards the horizon – like divine intervention, which always resolves human hardship.
Caravaggio accentuates the violent scene before him: in the foreground, the shiny knife becomes a protagonist of the scene. Directly next to it is the terrified face of the boy, similar to the street urchin painted by the artist some years earlier. The face and the inaudible scream are unforgettable and one of the first in Italian painting to display the scream of the abused boy.
With figures such as these, Caravaggio demonstrates his explosive expressiveness. The Biblical narrative becomes an expression of innocence and an attack against it, as well as a commentary on the steadfastness of faith. (Note the plasticity of Abraham's wrist.)
Through the integration of two asynchronous events (the scene of sacrifice and the discovery of the ram), a restrained dynamic comes into being, lending an exceptional vitality to the warm, protective color of Abraham's clothing. It accentuates the violent, sudden intervention of the divine into the lives of men, a

motif which is seen in other images by Caravaggio and which clearly magnifies the impact of the viewer's involvement.

In contrast to the previous image, the earlier version (1597–1598, Princeton, Piasecka-Johnson Collection) is much less violent. The youthful angel, in conversation with the ancient Abraham, shows him the ram. The facial expression of Isaac displays a mixture of resignation and surprise. The entire scene has an aura of peacefulness. The light stops at the face of the smiling angel, descends and breaks through the darkness, in order to shine upon various parts of Isaac's smooth body. This time, God's mercy makes its way unobtrusively, in an environment that is dominated more by stillness than by sound. Caravaggio emphasizes the familiarity of the conversation between the figures of Abraham and the angel-god, before the setting of a dark night illuminated solely by the miraculous visitation. Also clearly evident is the corporeal-theatrical and symbolic function of light, as a type of "word" accompanying the arrival of the divine.

2. David and Goliath

Oil on poplar wood, 90.5 x 116 cm. Vienna, Kunsthistorisches Museum.

The panel was executed in 1607 over a painting from the Cinquecento and depicts one of the most famous stories from the Old Testament (Samuel 1:17). In contrast to other artists, such as Michelangelo in a spandrel vault of the Sistine Chapel, Caravaggio does not depict the moment of David's beheading of Goliath, but the moment that follows, as the young man stands up and displays the head to the crowd. From the dark background, the athletic form of the hero emerges with his determined gaze, radiant in his triumphant certainty and yet aloof, distanced, lost in thoughts of gratitude to God, to whom he turned before the battle after Goliath openly ridiculed him for his youthfulness. The strong light, which illuminates the pouch and his upper body with the loose tunic, within which the folds seep into the shadows with a wonderful chiaroscuro effect, ultimately focuses upon the distorted contours of the open-mouthed Goliath – a shocking portrait of the artist. The inertia of the painting transforms it into a kind of vision of an event, one beyond space and time that fosters reflection. David becomes a symbol of youthful confidence, whose untarnished belief in God guides the narrative. Yet a profound drama is hidden within this work. On the one hand, the young man internalizes a victory that opens up a future still unknown to him; on the other hand, it is the suffering of the painter, who renders himself in the skin of a corpse and fearfully ponders his own death. Indeed, the years spent in various cities after fleeing Rome were his last. In the meantime, Caravaggio concentrates his style into extremes. His color palette includes only white, ocher, black, and gray, in order to allow for a maximum amount of chiaroscuro effects and at the same time, to escalate the narrative on a grand scale, implying that David, who rests the sword upon his shoulder, is also the presence of life who challenges death. Of this Biblical motif exist two additional versions by Caravaggio. The older one (1597–1598, now in Madrid, Prado Museum) displays the young man in a light-colored tunic with boldly articulated chiaroscuro. He has just severed Goliath's head and is in the process of lifting it from the ground. The profile view of David, framed by a slight shadow, shows that he is still breathless; the moonlight lingers upon his long arm and bare leg, accentuating his strong personality and determined character. In this work, Caravaggio underlines the power of mercy surrounding the young man who has been entrusted with a divine mission, while a marked contrast is created by the massive body

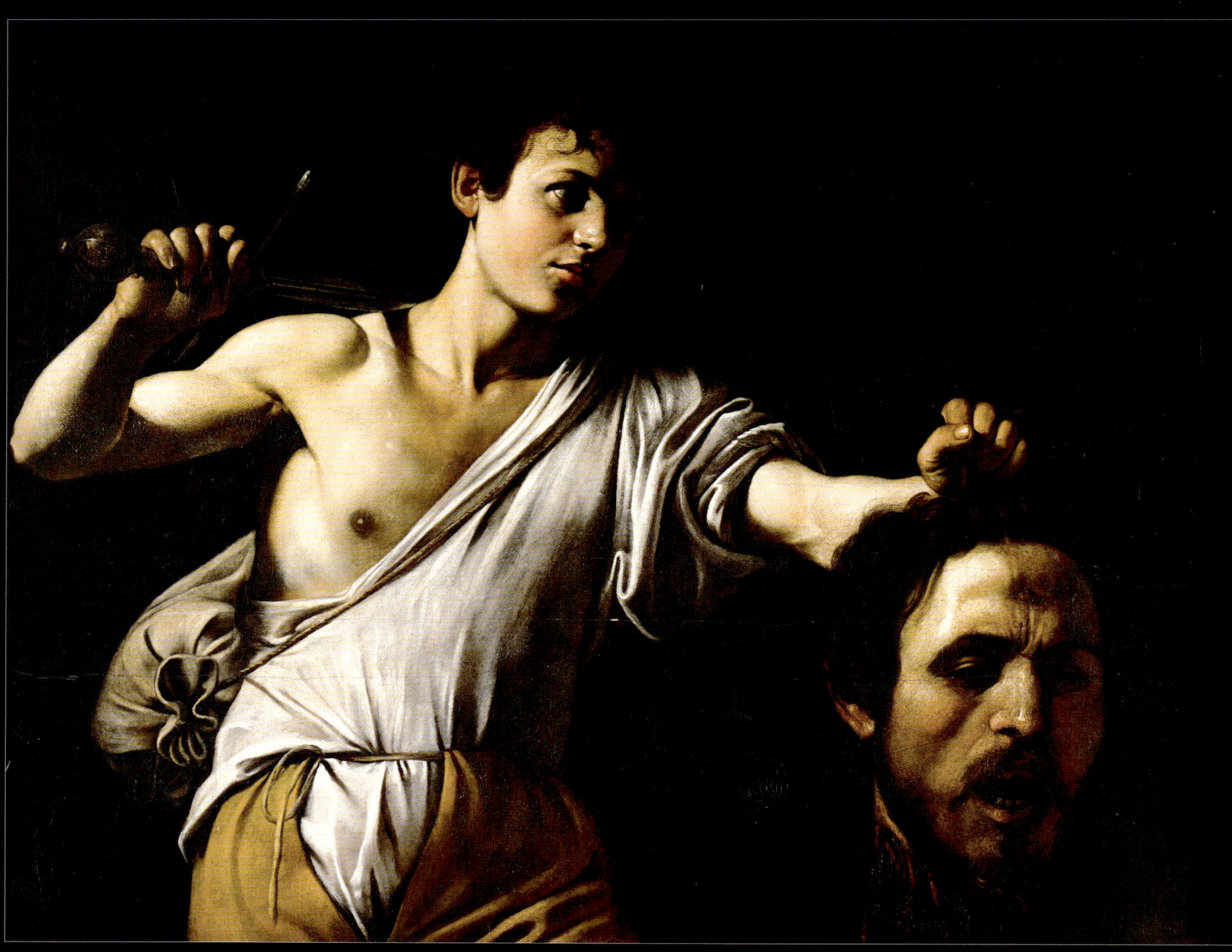

and enormous fist of the giant. Unlike its counterpart in Vienna, the "closeup" strengthens the narrative element with a thoroughly articulated contradiction between light and dark, which here too, blends into one another in the dark sections of the background. The third version of this subject may go back to 1610, the year in which Caravaggio died, and can be seen in the Roman Galleria Borghese. It was supposedly completed for Cardinal Borghese, in order to invoke papal forgiveness after Tomassoni's murder and is a truly heartbreaking confession. Particularly striking is the affinity between the personal and the Biblical story. A young, desperately unhappy David appears to reflect more upon the misery before him (which is mentioned in the ensuing Bible chapters) than the joy of his victory. He displays the disfigured face of Goliath, the last self-portrait of the artist after the attempt on his life in Naples by the Knights of Malta.

The image is more a monochromy in white and brown than it is a color painting. It is also a beseeched plea for forgiveness – Caravaggio renders himself twice: as a youth and as he later appeared – as well as a commentary on human desperation and fear of approaching death. In the story of David and Goliath, the painter recognizes a metaphor of personal significance and the life-death relationship that defined his (and every man's) existence. The two figures, both in the foreground, are immobilized like an icon of pain; they are fixed by a spotlight that casts a cold light upon the young man's face and chest and glances off a portion of Goliath's face. They recall the suffering of Grünewald's Crucifixion images or the desolation of a late Michelangelo.

Like the still, distressed David, Caravaggio nonetheless harbors the quiet hope that death does not have the last word.

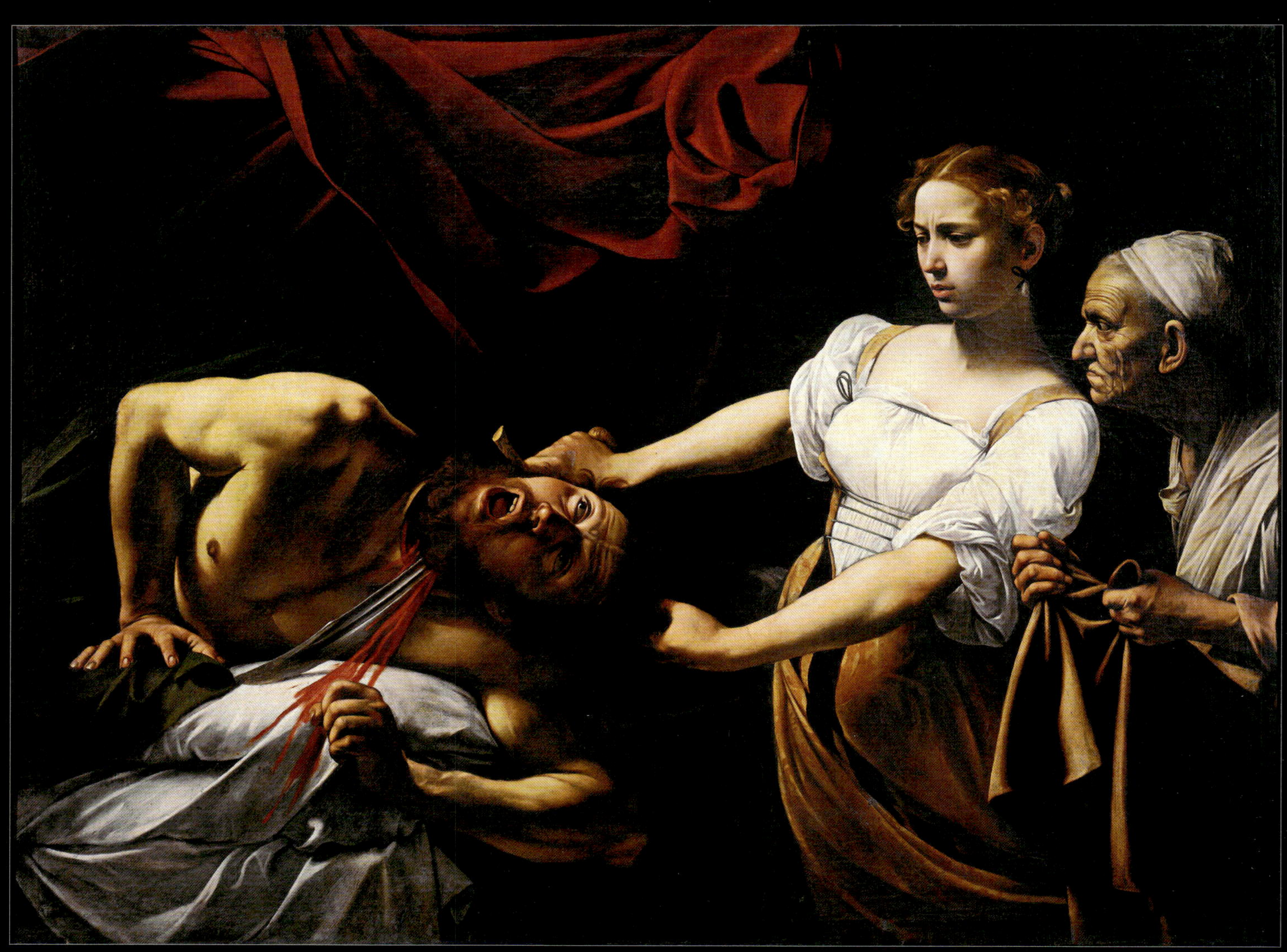

3. Judith and Holofernes

Oil on canvas, 144 x 195 cm. Rome, Galleria Nazionale di Arte Antica, Palazzo Barberini.

The painting was completed for the banker Ottavio Costa in 1599, when the painter entered the circle of Cardinal Del Monte, his protector.

The famous motif from the 13th chapter of the Book of Judith was represented in a myriad of ways over the course of centuries. Botticelli represents the heroine as she returned to the camp of the Israelites; he accentuated the beauty of the young, almost carefree and pensive woman at dawn, while the maid follows her with the head of Holofernes upon a tray. In the Sistine Chapel, Michelangelo depicts the moment at which Judith departs from the tent where the giant body of the decapitated enemy lies. In all cases, Judith is the symbol of female strength, faith in God, and liberation from oppression.

Caravaggio invents a highly theatrical, elaborately detailed representation, so as to create an impact and even incite revulsion in the viewer. Upon the horizontal canvas, the scene is placed before a large blood-red cloth, virtually a theater backdrop that the artist uses more and more frequently for heightened narrative effect. Strong light from the left falls upon Judith, who has just cut off the head of her enemy, and accentuates the pure white blouse of the young widow, her blond hair, and the muscular body of Holofernes, who

writhes in agonized pain. Blood spurts violently upon the pristine white sheet. At Judith's side, the old servant looks on in horror and extends her apron to receive the head.

Caravaggio's portrayal, in its lurid realism, is deliberately harsh and shocking, perhaps even recalling the open executions of that era. Just as deliberately, he emphasizes other, more peaceful elements of the Biblical story. Judith, with the solid beauty of Caravaggesque women, tense yet determined, is the self-aware instrument of divine justice, more so than the old woman – a female type frequently encountered in the artist's early paintings – who is present as an accomplice, but whose involvement in the event appears somewhat marginal.

The painter places weight upon the moral strength of the heroine, whose contours are also infused with a certain amount of fear. She becomes the allegory of radical life-and-death decisions for freedom, which always contains risk. However, the succinct light tells us that the narrative takes place beneath the eye of God.

With this image, Caravaggio begins a long series of violent representations with strongly dramatic effects, in which he grapples with the tragedies of life and the conflicts between pursuers and the pursued. He employs the Biblical stories as an occasion for its utterly singular meditations upon suffering. This is manifested in the theme of bloodshed that extends throughout his entire work, as evidenced by the constant use of blood-red pigment.

From the start, the canvas was immensely popular; it inspired and was frequently copied by Italian and European painters who did not grasp its notion of moral revolt against oppression, nor its concept of trust in a God who freed the people via the "weak" – youths such as David or women like Judith. However, painters who availed themselves to these templates only as a pretext for gruesome or emphatically dramatic scenes, succeeded in creating a truly pictorial genre.

Stories From the New Testament

Most of Caravaggio's Biblical subjects originate from the New Testament. In the life of Christ – which was dramatic from the outset – the painter locates a parallel, a clear correlation with human stories and their painful twists, even when the thread of hope never completely abandons the artist's thoughts. Sacred stories and human stories are in some ways congruent, not least of all because a certain sacredness is inherent to every human being.

Caravaggio's intuition is completely original, expressed according to a powerful exploration of emotions within a convincingly theatrical format, of a deep observation of every Gospel verse that the artist imbues with unique psychological and spiritual nuances.

His Bible of the poor and humiliated appear as a virtual film of the entire life cycle of man; in doing so, an adoring gaze also destroys the bloodiest moments. Christ becomes a human among humans – a man of suffering, but not only that. By means of the style characterized by chiaroscuro and an application of a color scale, ranging from an initial luminosity to the deep tones of later works, the words and deeds of Jesus become the voice of all humanity. This is the unique Christocentricism of Caravaggio; a new method by which to read and visually interpret the Gospel text. One could in fact say that for the "Catholic" Caravaggio, Christ is precisely God, for he is fully human.

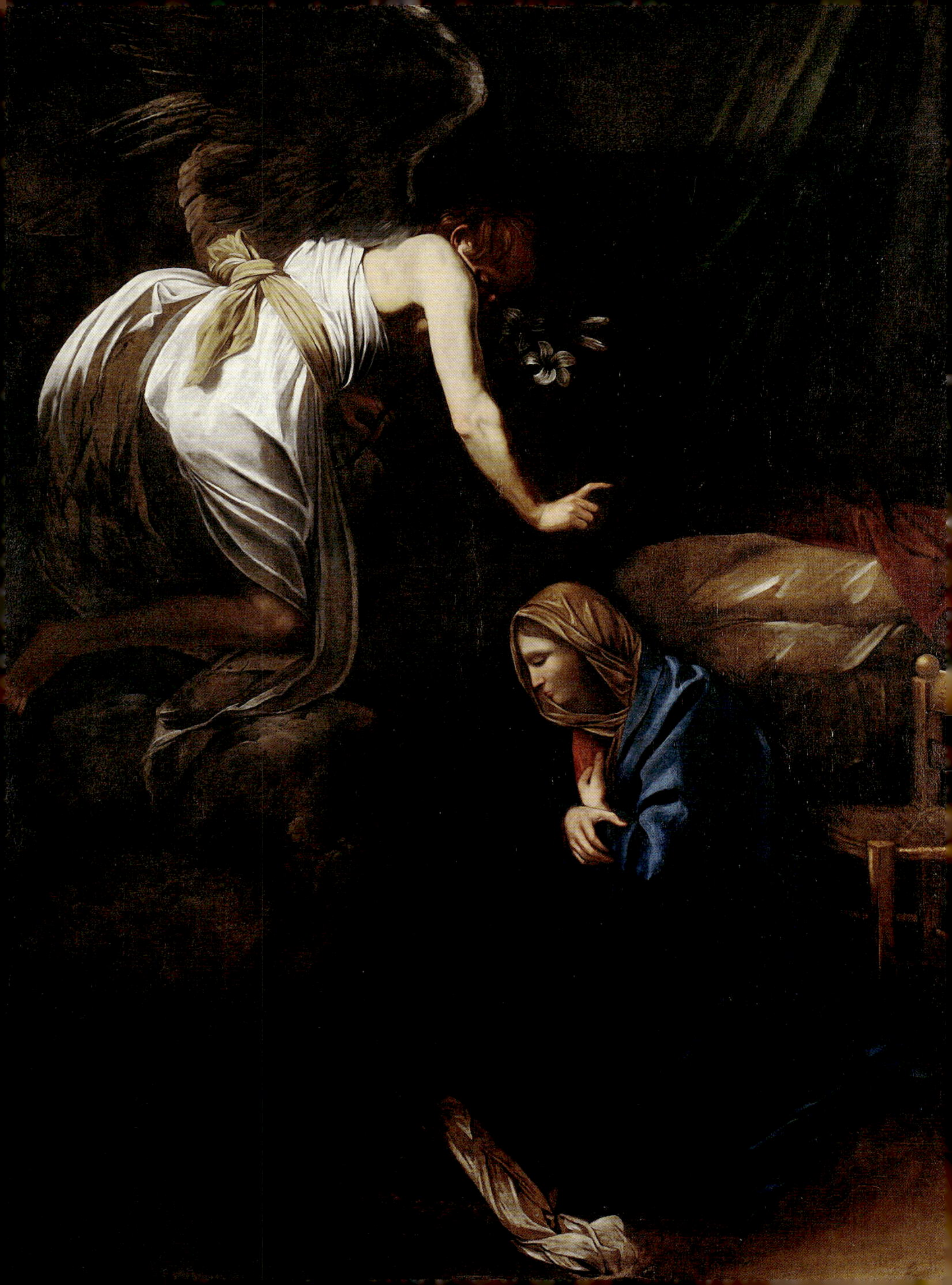

1. Annunciation

Oil on canvas, 285 x 205 cm. Nancy, Musée des Beaux-Arts.

The large canvas was painted in 1609 (perhaps in Malta) on behalf of Enrico II. di Lorena. The rapid brushstrokes, limited palette, and its human as well as spiritual depth reveal the master's late style. While Caravaggio takes on a traditional theme, his consolidation of the room, place, and narrative into a single entity is innovative.

The Virgin Mary, shown in profile, is absorbed deeply in prayer. The model for this figure also posed for Salome in the *Beheading of John the Baptist* in Malta. In a kneeling position, the Madonna listens to the message of a youthful angel, who bends from the cloud overhead in a forced pose of clearly Mannerist taste. One hand is extended in blessing; with the other, he holds a lily, the symbol of purity.

Between the two figures is an empty, wide, dark room; with this, the painter appears to indicate the "darkness" with which the Spirit overcomes the Virgin, as mentioned in the Gospel of Luke. The living area in which the scene takes place is rendered using few brushstrokes. We see the conventional curtain, an unmade bed, and a wicker stool. The scant furnishings and restrained colors unite this work with others from the Sicilian period, which are all infused with a strongly meditative sensibility and a "Franciscan" sparseness. Throughout his lifetime, Caravaggio felt drawn to the figure of the saint, represented him in three of his paintings, turning the economy of the painted medium at this point into an artistic language of the highest spirituality.

The azure blue of Mary's cloak, which is typical in scenes of the Annunciation, is quite restrained, with the basket and cloth set upon the ground contrasting only somewhat to the neutral shadow of the indistinct floor. Strangely, the angel is shown from the back, instead of in profile or from the front, and he too, appears more as a fleeting presence.

Caravaggio describes the moment of the event – typical for the "here and now" view of the age – focusing upon its decisive movements: the dynamic of the messenger (recalling the *Annunciation* by Lorenzo Lotti in Recanati), the gentle acceptance of the Virgin, with her hands upon her breast, and the hazy presence of a scant number of objects, appearing as earth-toned phantoms within the solitary room. One could say that the painter captured the Virgin's surprise, but also her immediate reply, incorporating diverse moments (annunciation, fear, response) into a few gestures that have been reduced to their essentials. The angel's gesture is decisive, that of the Madonna is composed. It is again the theme of one's calling, whose sublime beauty and depth the painter had already addressed in the *Conversion On the Way to Damascus* and in *The Calling of Saint Matthew*. Here for the last time, he considers the Virgin's acquiescence, almost as if he wished to complete a thematic cycle. We notice Merisi's extraordinary ability to describe the Virgin's soul that is similar to the images of the Madonna in Naples or Sicily. Each time, when he chooses a main female character, he allows a sentimental and placid tenderness to emerge. Here too, it is evident in the hazy atmosphere in which Maria, her heart pounding, gives her consent to the divine summons.

The image becomes a painted, restrained, and devout prayer, like all those by Caravaggio that include the Virgin Mary. In comparison, the works of his major contemporaries such as Annibale Carracci or Federigo Barocci may seem appealing and of a popular piety. However, they lack the spiritual finesse that Caravaggio has invested into the narrative, making it tangible and accessible to us.

2. Birth of Christ

Oil on canvas, 268 x 197 cm. Formerly Palermo, Oratorio di San Lorenzo.

The painting was stolen in 1969 and has not been rediscovered since. Caravaggio painted it between August and October of 1609, making it his last work in Sicily. The image, which demands a complex reading, was commissioned by the Compagnia di San Francesco in Palermo, although it is not clear whether the painter went there or had it sent to the patron from Messina. The saints Francis and Lawrence are seen in contemplative poses along the edges of the painting, while Saint Joseph, appearing as an old farmer with a hat and a herd behind him, is shown observing the scene.

The dominating impression is that of a familiar, peaceful, "sacra conversazione." One might argue that it is consistent with Lombard tastes, one of those surprising respites of the painter over the course of his very turbulent life. The Mother of God sits upon the ground, as in the Byzantine representations of the Nativity, and gazes at the child at her feet. She has completely retreated into herself, exhibiting a deeply personal wonder reminiscent of Correggio's renowned *Annunciation* (Florence, Uffizi).

The themes of poverty and humility, which were typical of the Capuchins' spiritual milieu and which Caravaggio often incorporated into his paintings, become the protagonists in this case. Still, the colors are lavish, the brush emphasizing the gold of the dalmatica of Saint Lawrence, who rests upon his attribute of the gridiron. There is also the red corsage of the mother and the yellow of the straw, upon which lies the completely naked child (as a prefiguration of the Passion). The stable, in keeping with traditional iconography, is bathed in warm light. There are the ox and shepherd seen from the back, the light marvelously playing upon the latter's gray hair; he converses with Joseph, who bears the kind features of the farmer. The two saints are clothed differently: Francis stands off to the side in the dark, his hands folded and clothed in the brown habit of the Order; Lawrence, the portrait of a contemporary of the artist, gazes at the child, lost in thought.

Light falls from above, brought by an angel holding a scroll with the words, "Gloria in Eccelsis Deo." The light flows upon the the Madonna's face and breast, and is cast upon the shepherd and parts of Saint Lawrence, so as to concentrate upon the small face of the child. It is the path between heaven and earth, whose bridge becomes the Virgin Mary placed in the middle. She is the connection between the two dimensions, emphasizing her function as the intermediary for Christ, God incarnate.

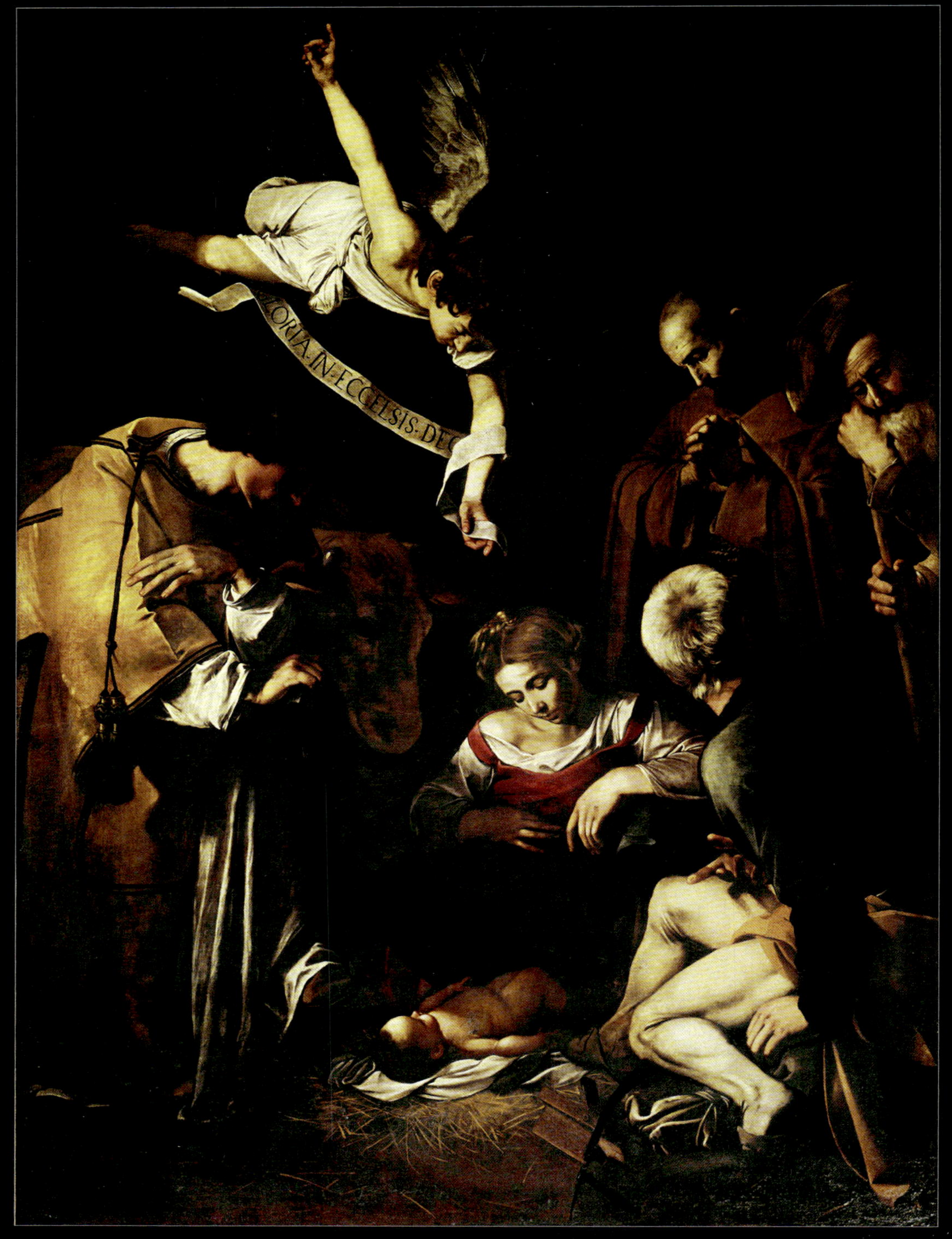

...ORIA IN ECCLESIS DE...

The painting is constructed as an ordered, peacefully scenic grouping and centers upon the Virgin Mary and her ordinary face as a woman of the people. Her hands are diversely arranged: the right rests upon her abdomen, which has just given birth; in a humble gesture, the other hand shows the saints the "fruit of her womb"(Gospel of Luke), namely the Christ child. The image radiates a feeling of peace and joy in worship that is reflected in its warm hues.

In the same year, Caravaggio painted *The Adoration of the Shepherds* (oil on canvas, 314 x 211 cm., Messina, Museo Regionale) for the main altar of the Capuchin Church, Santa Maria della Consolazione in Messina. Here too, it is also the Gospel of Luke which is referenced through the artist's simple, elaborately-shaded painting. The setting is the traditional stable with animals and shepherds, who vacillate between surprise and adoration. The seated Joseph, old and wizened, gazes at his young wife. In a moment of utter intimacy with her child, the artist paints her lying down in the Byzantine tradition of the Madonna of Humility. This group of figures is considered to be one of the most poetic moments in the art of Caravaggio, who is captivated by the love between mother and son. The two faces nestled closely to one another are painted in a vibrant chiaroscuro that also illuminates the shadowed surroundings, and the "sparseness" of the pigments (white, red and yellow) becomes further intensified by their lucidity.

The stable wall in the background is high; one can virtually smell the wood and the straw, painted stalk by stalk to create an atmosphere of simple meditation, in which the artist portrays these simple folk with affection. It is a nativity of the people, for they are meant to immediately receive the message of the Gospel, offered to them in a simple, truthful language. The diffused light expresses a trace of melancholy, as if Caravaggio had sadly recalled the joy of a family who had abandoned him during this difficult period of his life.

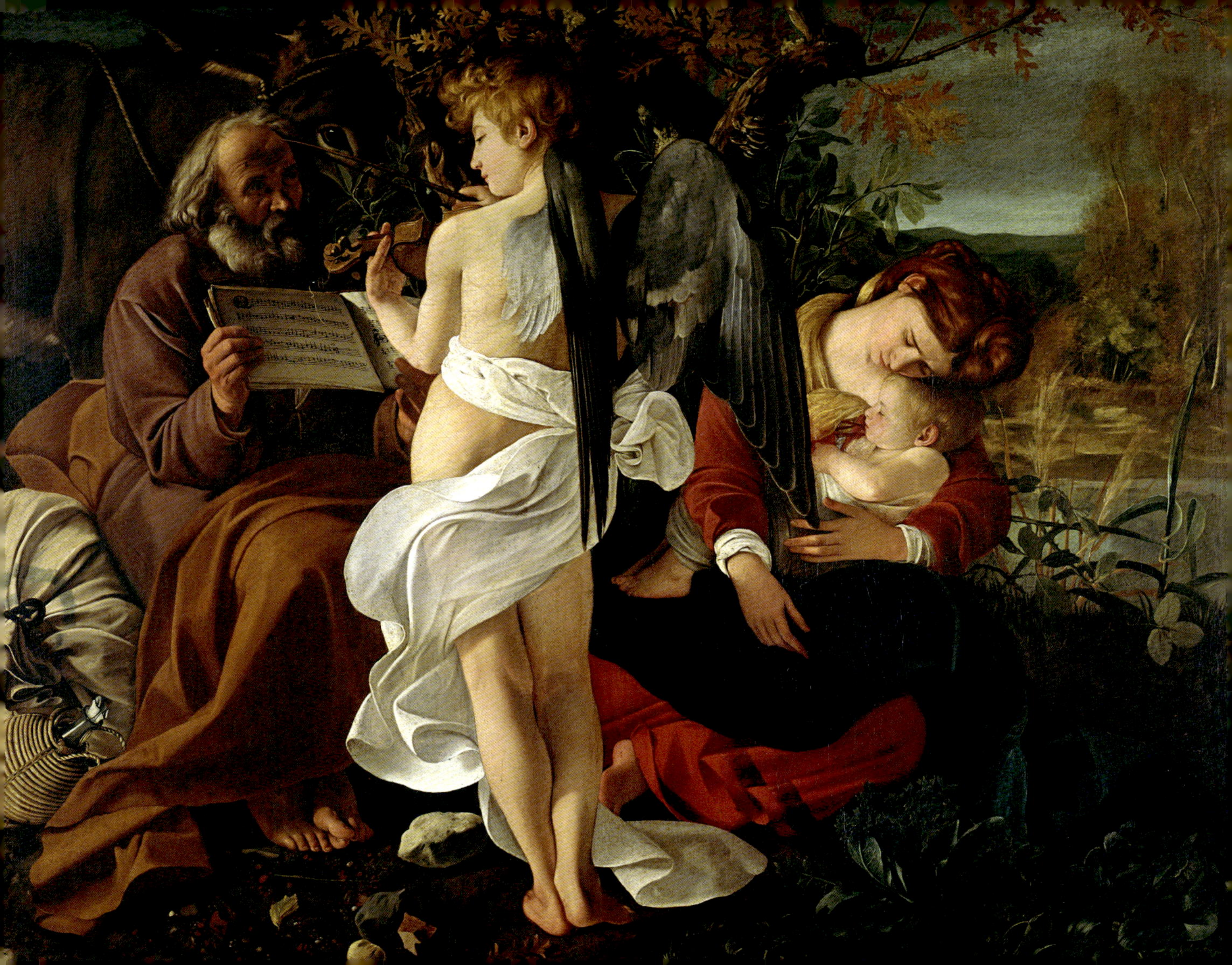

3. Rest on the Flight to Egypt

Oil on canvas, 133.5 x 166.5 cm. Rome, Galleria Doria Pamphilj.

The subject is based upon the story of the Holy Family's escape to Egypt, as told in the Gospel of Mark. It gave many artists the opportunity to compose pastoral-tranquil domestic scenes, such as the buoyant image by Federigo Barocci in the Vatican Pinakothek.

In this early work (1595–1596) commissioned by the Aldobrandini family, Caravaggio again takes up the motif of his profane illustrations of young fruit sellers or still lifes and inserts them into a rustic setting, using countless details to describe a moment of respite during the Holy Family's escape.

The entire image radiates an aura of peace; it is open and full of light. The mother, from sheer weariness, has fallen asleep with her child in her arms, Saint Joseph sits upon his bag and holds open the music for the violin-playing angel, while a donkey follows the scene, his gaze watchful.

Based upon the plant life, the painting shows an autumn scene. The landscape extends to the horizon with the veiled dawn, suggesting a Lombard sky. Leaves, flowers, and stones upon the ground are painted with immense precision and love of detail. The entire image emanates a simple and moving natural poetry. In doing so, Caravaggio particularly appears to have had Lorenzo Lotto in mind. Reminiscent of this artist are the youthful angel with his sleek body and soft wings with swallow tail ends, as well as the elegant arrangement of the folds, that are moved by the wind, which in turn emphasizes the white, while the profile of Caravaggio's young model refers to other paintings. The Madonna is also influenced by certain precedents of Venetian-Lombard painting. However, the painter places a unique accent upon the representation of the sleeping pair – mother and son – with an empathy and subtlety that is only seen again in the later *Birth of Christ* from Messina. It is a humble world – Joseph bears the features of a weary laborer – in which the divine is revealed and becomes part of daily life. Everything is real: the musical score of a verse from the Biblical song to honor the Virgin Mary, "Quam pulchra es et quam decora" by the Franco-Flemish musician Noel Bauldeweyn, the violin, the tracks of the wagon wheels (located on the way to Egypt, perhaps at an oasis), and the plants, such as the mullein at the Mother of God's feet, which often appears in Caravaggio's Christological paintings and amounts to immortality in the medieval language of symbols.

However, the description of the environment in which the scene takes place is not an end in itself. Caravaggio expresses a deeply internalized reality of man, which is also a "social" motif in the present case, a quasi-dissipation of the Magnificat from the Gospel of Luke, in which God "exalted them of low degree." This mentality was widespread at the time of Catholic reform, especially in the Franciscan circles and Oratorians of Saint Philipp Neri. The latter put on many theatrical shows with religious subjects, which closely correlates to the painting under discussion.

At the same time, the painting contains a mystical element accentuated by the figure of the angel. The youth, who appears to come from another world and plays a passage of amorous and mystical ardor, represents a unifying element of sorts: between the everyday, which is familiar with exertion and the need for respite – we are always in a situation of "escape" – and the reality of a divine presence (that is, the angel) that accompanies mankind, offering respite and providing solace with heavenly music. The beauty of this divine music is reflected by the light, which illuminates the child's face as well as his mother, who protectively embraces him with utmost tenderness.

Perhaps such images fulfill the painter with longing for the mother he lost at a young age, and why in each treatment of the Virgin Mary, he consistently discovers unique nuances of warmheartedness, as if this figure represented to him the epitome of peace and security.

4. John the Baptist (John in the Wilderness)

Oil on canvas, 94 x 131 cm. Rome, Galleria Nazionale d'Arte Antica, Palazzo Corsini.

The figure of the Baptist appears in all four Gospels and consistently remained a popular motif in art. Here, we see a version from 1605 which, in keeping with the typical iconography of that period, shows the saint in the wilderness.

The painter uses a young boy for his model, like others such as Andrea del Sarto (Florence, Palazzo Pitti), in order to achieve the most natural illustration possible of a young man. Along the rectangular canvas, we see John sitting at an angle, with a bowl and staff as symbols of his ascetic way of life. His face is enveloped in shadow. Caravaggio painted him with decisive brushstrokes full of light – a prefiguration of Velàzquez.

The shadow, which surrounds the Baptist, allows for the hairless chest, the white loincloth, and the red cloak bathed in light to stand out even more prominently. As in other representations of youth, John is invested with the fascination of an undemonstrative, isolated, almost unapproachable adolescence, as if the spotlight which exposes his body and especially his shoulder, irritated him. This John flees from companionship, not being accustomed to friendship. Caravaggio pauses at the gracious countenance with the voluminous head of hair; he reads the thoughts of the young prophet, whose flawless body shows no signs of future self-chastisement. He may have been depicted during a moment of respite on his way to the desert, pensive and surrounded by things that are lost in the dark. However, his decision is already made, with the decisiveness of young heroes who pause only briefly before fulfilling their plans.

Appearing in a version from approximately 1597 attributed to Caravaggio (oil on canvas, 169 x 112 cm., Toledo, Museo Tesoro Catedralico) is a youth with adolescent features: in some Biblical translations, it says that John "lived his early years in the desert." His face lies in shadow; he is clothed with the standard attributes (fur and red cloak), has a lamb next to him, while in the background, grapevines (the blood of Christ) and a twig from a bramble bush (the crown of thorns) can be seen. Here, too, the painter confronts us with an unusual atmosphere of placidity and childlike tranquility, which is further sustained by the lamb, a symbol of compliance.

In around 1604, a version of *John the Baptist* was executed, now in Kansas City (oil on canvas, 173 x 133 cm., Nelson-Atkins Museum of Art). Beneath a cold light, the full-portrait figure of the young saint is clearly distinguished from the background. The

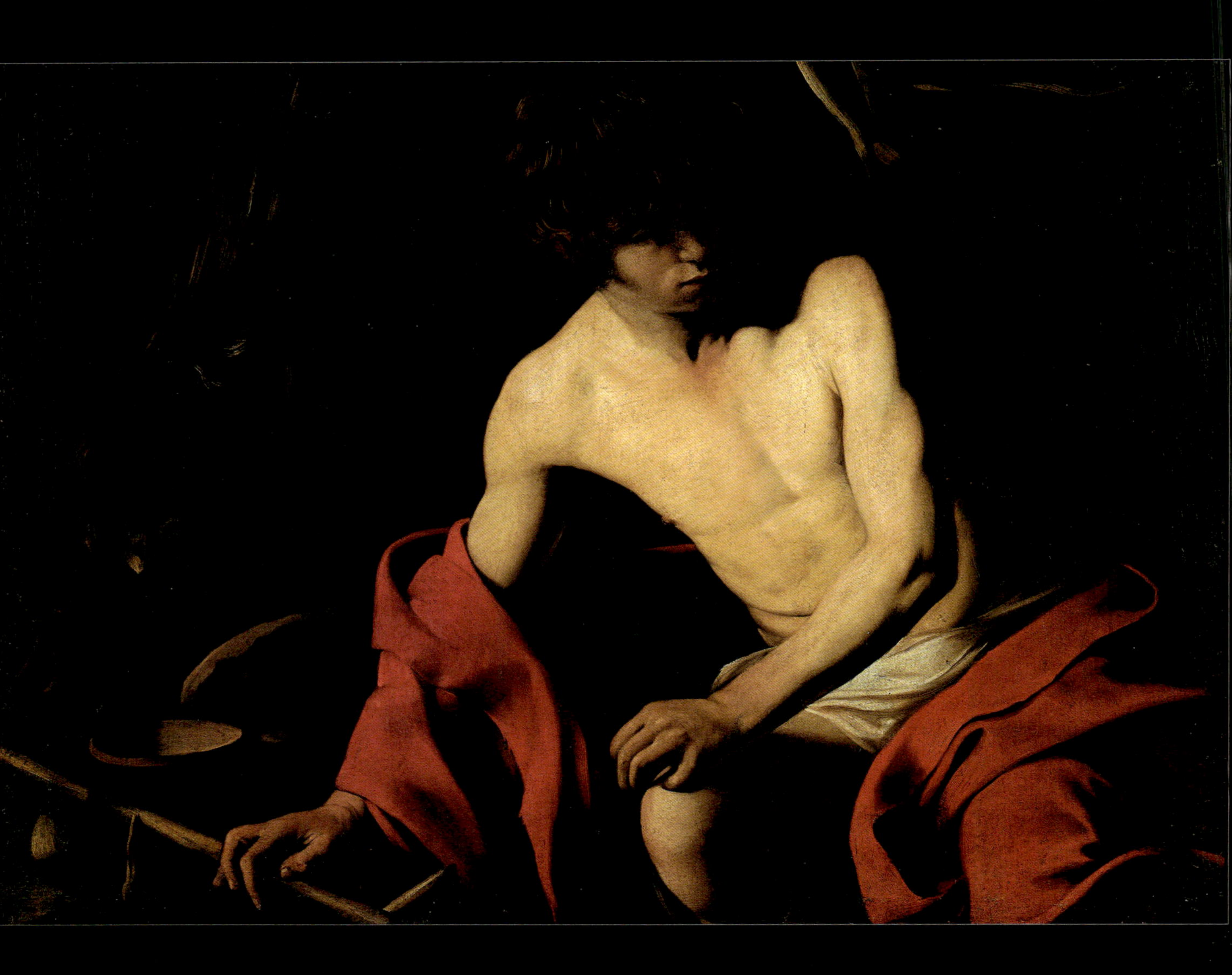

surroundings consist of a large tree with numerous dry leaves. John appears to glower with the look of a young man who seems to have experienced a great deal, his gaze becoming lost in the darkness. His pose with outspread legs suggests that he is about to get up again, or that he has only sat down for a brief moment. The theatricality of the scene is highlighted by a widely spread cloak which bisects the canvas, its luminous pigment infusing the atmosphere with tension.

It is possible that the *Youth With a Ram* in Rome's Musei Capitolini (1602, oil on canvas, 131 x 98.6 cm.) may not even be John the Baptist, but rather, the rescued Isaac. The pose is that of a Michelangelo-esque *ignudo* from the Sistine Chapel, who expresses a terrestrial life force and an unrestrained delight, even laying aside his white and red clothing to embrace the ram. Caravaggio accentuates the sensuality of the youth's body, modeled from chiaroscuro, and conjures up a self-satisfied smile upon the not-handsome, but expressively strong face. The (alleged) Baptist symbolizes youthful vitality, with an abandon similar to the heroes painted by the Carraccis in the Roman Galleria Farnese.

From 1609–1610 comes a painting that currently hangs in the Galleria Borghese in Rome (oil on canvas, 159 x 124 cm.). Caravaggio chooses a boy with a childish appearance; his body limp, with the red cloak next to him. As an allusion to the sacrifice of Christ, he appears before a background of wine leaves. In the place of a lamb, a ram appears in the painting, possibly in reference to the sacrifice of Isaac, who John thought to be the last prophet of the Old Testament. The overall impression of the painting is melancholy, which in spite of the perfectly articulated chiaroscuro accents in the lines of the body, is further emphasized through color. The boy's face, with his black shimmering eyes, prophesizes sadness (John says with regard to Jesus, "He must increase, but I must decrease"). This melancholia is also justifiable, as the painter finds himself nervously awaiting a papal pardon. The image, one of the master's last, appears to be his spiritual testament. It is an act of love in relation to life, whose disappearance he fears.

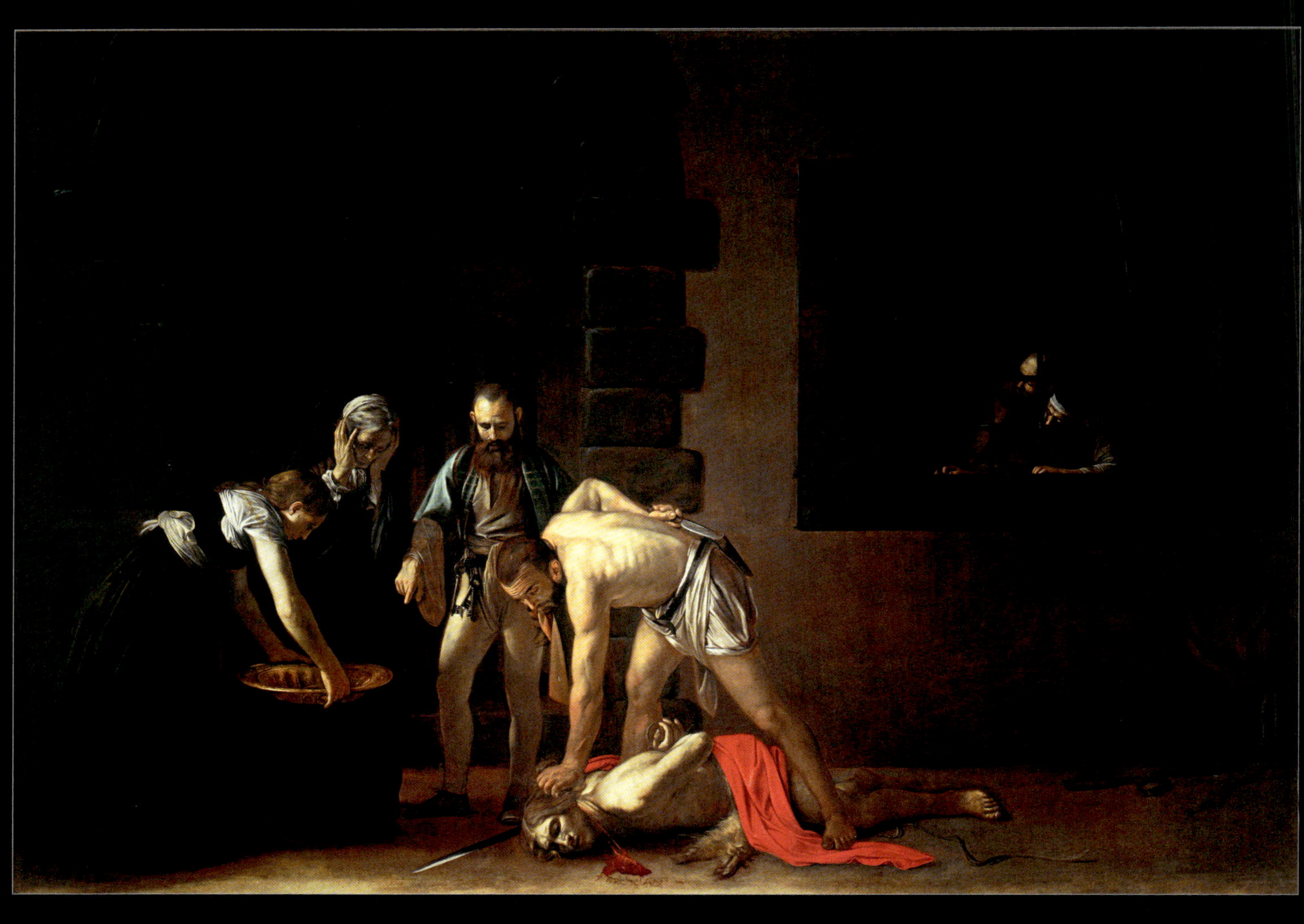

5. The Beheading of John the Baptist

Oil on canvas, 361 x 520 cm. Malta, La Valletta, Co-Cathedral St. John, Oratorium.

The largest painting by Caravaggio originated in Malta in 1608 and is one of the highest expressions not only of his art, but among European art history as a whole. The universally known story from the Gospel is reflected from an entirely new angle. The theme of abandonment becomes increasingly important to the artist and to his images, virtually echoed by Jesus' cry upon the cross, who feels that God is far away from him. In this instance, it is the prophet (humanity) who appears to have been cast off to a cruel death. After the beheading, the executioner applies a finishing stroke with the knife. Indeed, the painter was a fugitive at the time and felt this sword of Damocles hover above him.

Typical for Sicilian images, the scene is positioned at the left of the canvas, creating a large empty space on the right side. The group of figures, who experience the tragic event in diverging ways, stand across from the desolate space of this emptiness, almost as an escalating scream of death into eternity: the void of solitude of every man in death and the answer which fails to materialize.

The colors intensify into luminous red, white, and green nuances. The four figures are also frozen in photograms of gruesomeness, oppressed by the reality of death: the jailer, who proclaims judgment, the endlessly sad executioner, who is shown sharpening his knife, with features appearing as a variation of the artist's self-portrait, Salome, who hurries forth with a basin to hold the severed head, and the old woman, who clutches her head in desperation and pity. From a distance behind bars, two prisoners observe the fate which lies ahead of them.

The light, which originates from various sources, attempts to make its way between the shadows along the high prison walls, finally meeting John, in a blood-red mantle in the foreground. Again, the theme of blood appears, and it is worth noting that Caravaggio places his only signature in the trail of blood beneath the martyr's head: fear, premonition, cognizance of the drama of his life?

Holy, personal, and human stories fully coincide. The image presents a tragic view of the world, sparing neither artist nor saint and appearing upon the canvas with utterly skillful expressiveness. This power is reminiscent of the great writers of Greek tragedies, reappearing in artists such as Rembrandt and Goya. Here, it is Caravaggio's poetic inspiration which gives its voice to innocent pain and the righteous who have suffered martyrdom through human injustice everywhere. Thus, Saint John's death becomes the death of every man who fights for freedom and integrity of the spirit. He becomes the voice of that part of humanity which rises above the coldness of the prison guard and Salome's revenge, continuing to believe in justice, to which the Baptist dedicated his life. It is that glimmer of faith which explains the gesture of the old woman and her pity, for it is this with which Caravaggio regards human history and the evil that shrouds persecutors and victims, but as evidenced by the serenity in the face of the dying John, is not the final word.

This theme is explored in greater detail in the painting *Salome with the Head of John the Baptist* (116 x 140 cm., Madrid, Palacio Real), one of the artist's last works (1609).

The image is a somber meditation on death, focusing upon the tense-looking Salome in the foreground. She wears the red mantle of the Baptist, whose head lays upon the basin. An old servant is painted in dark colors on a dark ground: injustice becomes the darkness of the soul. The executioner, who is seen from the back, appears indifferent and/or somber. The figures, who materialize from the dark background, radiate a monumental stillness; they are tragic illustrations of life suddenly interrupted by death. There is no joy in Salome, who does not savor her revenge at all, but instead, displays the grim sadness of evil.

Caravaggio painted an image with the same subject in 1607 (oil on canvas, 91.5 x 106.7 cm., London, National Gallery). Salome looks to the side, the executioner places the head upon a tray, an old woman observes. Each one displays a significant real and spiritual distance from the event, as if they had answered to an unavoidable fate. From this also comes the sense of fatality which catches the viewer off guard. The executioner, who resembles the painter, is illuminated by a decisive chiaroscuro, which carves out the figures like unreal apparitions. Death is in the present and the people are led to him by a violence which engulfs the light. The only relaxed face is that of the Baptist, whose open mouth has just exhaled his last breath.

6. Mary Magdalene

Oil on canvas, 122.5 x 98.5 cm. Rome, Galleria Doria Pamphilj.

Originally, the early work from 1594–1595 for the Aldobrandini family may have been intended to be a portrait of a girl drying her hair. Later, the artist changed the theme, referring to it as "The Calling" or "Invocation," a subject which frequently surfaces in Caravaggio's works. This constitutes the first example. Mary Magdalene is a popular figure in art, being identified as the sinner (or as Maria, the sister of Lazarus) who dried Jesus' feet with her hair, as told by the canonical and apocryphal Gospels.

This image presents her during her "conversion" or "calling." However, the latter is more appropriate, for the painter actually succeeded in capturing and expressing the intimate, highly personal circumstances and emotions of this moment.

The saint sits alone in a room diagonally illuminated by a light which shines upon part of the soft face, breast, and sumptuous damask material. She is dressed in the manner of a rich courtesan; the colors are warm and capture a great deal of light; the long, red hair falls loosely past her shoulders. The woman contemplates her life or more accurately, listens to an inner voice. Caravaggio describes the atmosphere of the collection, the internal dialogue of the woman, in a way that we can practically read her thoughts. Upon the ground are accoutrements of her past life: pearls, jewelery, a jar with oil which would be used to anoint the feet of Christ, made to shine by the entering ray of light. The jar could also refer to her love for Christ, in accordance with an interpretation of the Bible's Song of Songs.

With sparse, simple elements, the painter sketches this moment in the life of Mary Magdalene, trapped in this room, in which even the tile pattern is revealed by the light, barely indicating the room's spatial depth. Mary Magdalene lowers her gaze in a pensive manner; by contrast and as outlined by Saint Augustine, the light assumes the symbolic meaning of mercy in opposition to the darkness of sin.

With an absolute economy of devices and natural simplicity, Caravaggio blends material and moral reality.

An additional version exists of this work: *Martha and Mary* (oil on canvas, 100 x 134.5 cm., Detroit, Institute of Arts), painted in 1598. The scene shows Mary Magdalene (who is mistaken for the sinner of another episode from the Gospels) in conversation with her sister Martha. Martha – for whom the model was Fillide Melandroni, a friend of the artist – wears Venetian clothing and holds a small orange blossom, a

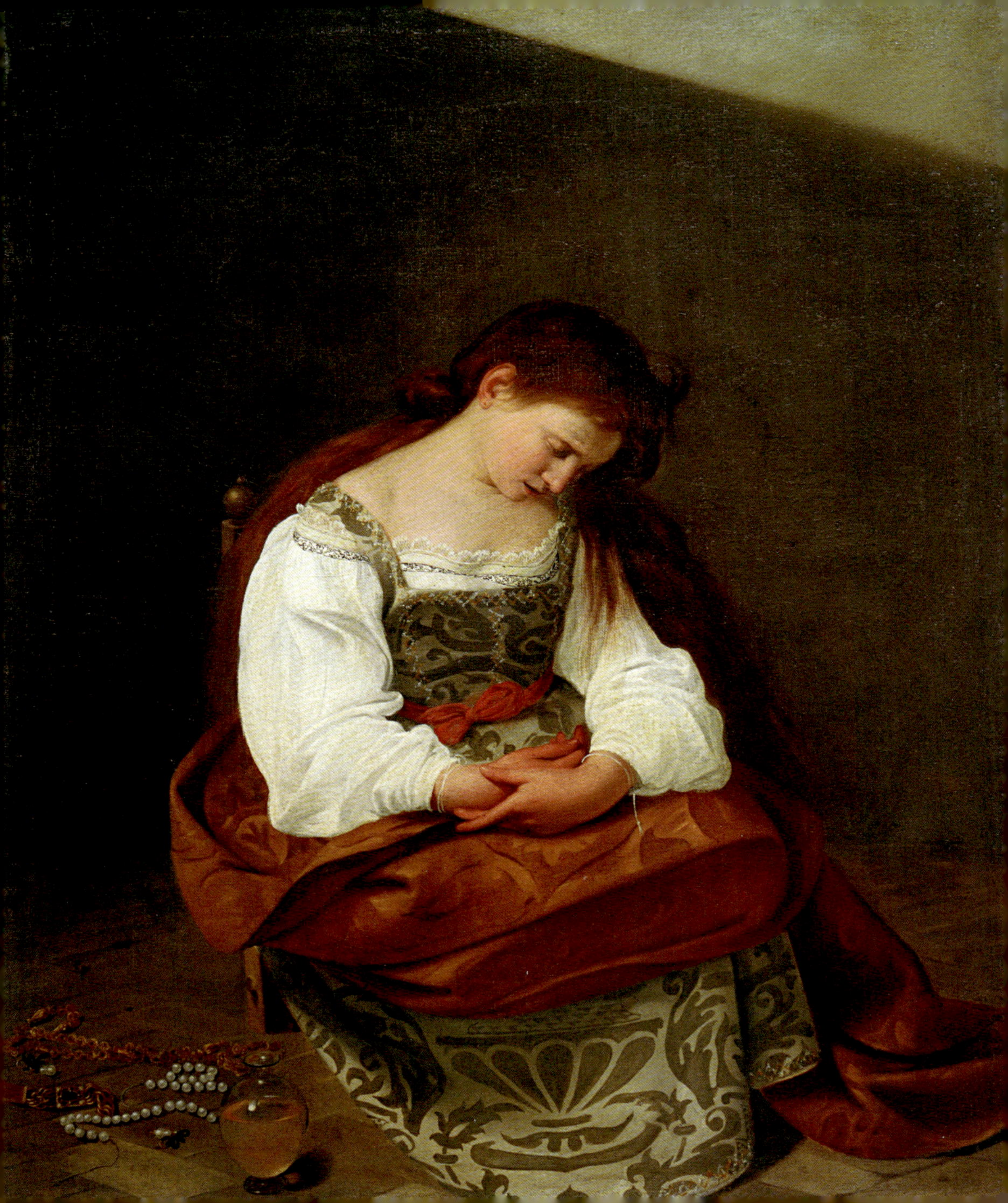

symbol of the marriage with Christ, at her breast. With the other hand, she points to a mirror that captures a strong beam of light (grace). The background remains neutral and typical of the works of Caravaggio, is painted using broad strokes without preliminary sketches. The pigments are lavish, almost luxurious.

Within the room is a certain air of worldliness, expressed in the objects upon the otherwise empty table, such as the ivory comb or the bowl and with sponge. The animated discussion between the sisters, however, suggests that it involves a moment in which a return to a new life will be decided.

Presaged in this painting is the future dominance of the dark-light relationship, one which will soon find highly dramatic expression. However, it remains moderate here due to the blaze of pigments, recalling Venetian art as well as the works of Dosso Dossi.

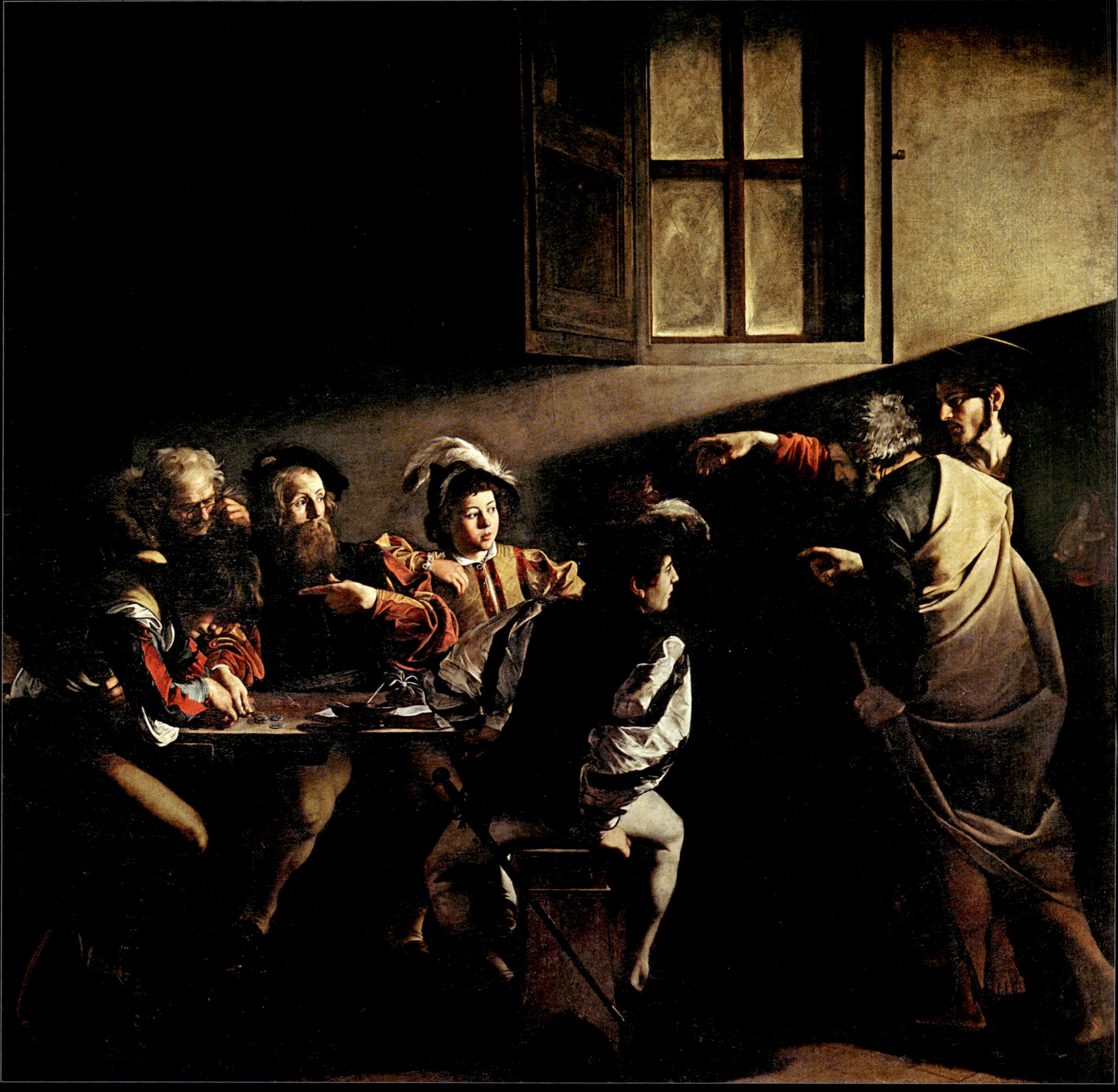

7. The Calling of Saint Matthew

The large panel was painted between 1599 and 1600 for the Contarelli Chapel. It is Caravaggio's first public work of its kind and was made possible by Cardinal de Monte. The painting stirred up admiration and controversy.

The story, which is only briefly mentioned in the synoptic Gospels but nonetheless frequently depicted by artists, takes on a uniquely beautiful, spectacular, and spiritual meaning with Caravaggio. In a tavern, where men are playing dice, Christ suddenly appears with a ray of light (grace) from an unseen window, where Matthew hesitates, while various light fragments extract other figures from the shadows. With psychological assertiveness and with rich Venetian colors, Caravaggio describes the world of those who are either not called upon or remain indifferent to grace. An astoundingly diverse human comedy ensues: unforgettable figures such as the bespectacled old man who looks at the results of the game, the disheveled younger man who greedily counts the money, the nobleman, who hurriedly scrambles to his feet at Jesus' entrance, the youth with the feather cap and placid face, who leans gently against the older man and is also captured by the light (perhaps the "young rich man" from the Gospel?).

Everything takes place within a large, darkened space with closed windows, high walls and an empty, presumably smoky room. With this, the painter wishes to say that a calling can take place anywhere, even within a tavern. The darkness epitomizes the unfathomableness (also in an internal sense) of the people, whose individual actions are captured with a strong sense of theatricality.

The dramatic event of the unexpected calling – which the artist had already considered in *Mary Magdalene* – is explored in a new way. The tall, slender Christ points to Matthew using a movement of the hand suggesting Michelangelo's *The Creation of Adam* in the Sistine Chapel. Its significance is subtle: in that image, it involved the calling of man to being; in this painting, it concerns the calling by God-turned-man, Christ, towards a new life. The new creation of this calling, in fact, converts man into another person, one who responds to grace. Matthew points to himself with a questioning glance: the calling is an answer to an invitation which comes from an outside source, in this case, from Christ, who is accompanied by Peter. Added at a later time, he with his staff refers to the pilgrimaging church in history, for within it, new life begins for those who have been called.

The light is no longer scattered, but focused, providing the painting with an emotional quality and endowing particular significance to every detail: from the table with coins to the items of clothing, to the psychological and dynamic contrasts that are charged with strong moral tension. The painting was used for decades as a model and in terms of its density and poetical heights, approaches the great dramas of Shakespeare, while simultaneously offering a new, deeper interpretation of the Bible text.

In the other images for the Contarini Chapel, Caravaggio did not achieve this concise power. In the *Martyrdom of Saint Matthew* which he first painted, he arranged a violent, almost excessively dynamic homicide. The painting is dominated by large, half-naked executioners, who have just killed the saint, and one screaming altar boy, who has become famous as an illustration of horror. They are the two faces of a tragedy, that additional figures witness with dismay and confusion: from the barely-clad young men at the baptismal font shown in Mannerist poses, to Caravaggio's contemporaries, among which he has depicted himself in the man standing between the columns thoughtfully observing the scene. The crowding and the dynamic contrast that are reminiscent of Tintoretto's paintings in the Scuola Grande di San Rocco (Venice) assume the significance of a rhetorically convincing, religious theater. The faithful should clearly realize that a martyr's death is possible.

For the area above the altar of the chapel, the painter completed *Saint Matthew and the Angel* (p. 14), moreover, in two different versions. The first version, which fell victim to fire in Berlin in 1945, did not satisfy the patron and was rejected on account of the clumsy rendering of Matthew, who appears with dirty feet and a Socrates-like face. The surviving 1602 version calls to mind a painting of the same name for the church S. Giovanni Evangelista in Brescia: we see the saint in ancient robes upon a wobbly footstool and a youthful angel. Clad in a snow-white cloth moved by the wind, he recites the first sentences of his Gospel, that is, the ancestral line of Jesus. As in the other paintings of the chapel, Caravaggio also modeled the figures in such a way here that they engage the viewer all at once – descend upon him, which was unprecedented for this period.

8. The Raising of Lazarus

Oil on canvas, 380 x 275 cm. Messina, Museo Regionale.

This painting was given to the Genoan merchant Giovan Battista de' Lazzeri on June 10, 1609 for the Chiesa dei Crociferi in Messina. It portrays the story from the 11th chapter of the Gospel of John.
In comparison to earlier forms of the theme (such as the monumental, densely populated scene by Sebastiano del Piombo in the London National Gallery), Caravaggio strikes out in an entirely new direction. As we have often ascertained in the later works of the artist, the image that is actually intended to express great joy is in fact pervaded by a boldly dramatic mood. Again, the painter concentrates upon the theme of death and its opposition to life, with the shock and hope that it provokes in every human being, focusing his inquiry upon the figure of Lazarus.
An actual corpse served as the model for the dead man, which clearly led to controversy. Lazarus is suspended in the limbo between eternal sleep and awakening. His outstretched arms, resembling a cross and referring to the soon-to-be crucified Jesus, do not capture much of the light which falls from the left, cutting through the nearly midnight darkness of the tomb. Above the group, a yawning void symbolizes death. The light illuminates Lazarus' shroud, his face, and that of his sister Mary directly above him. It is a stirring moment, in which the painter captures the painful affection of the sister with an unprecedented intensity.
The group of figures around the dead man fighting for his life, diligently attempts to follow the instructions of the powerful figure of Christ. His gestures are suggestive of *The Calling of Saint Matthew*, so as to demonstrate that Lazarus also involves the call to a new life. Christ appears like an apparition who has suddenly materialized, and the gazes of several figures are directed towards the entrance through which light virtually flows.
Remarkable is the row of "severed" heads above the arm of the Messiah. They are portraits of the various reactions of humanity that is stunned by the miracle before them. Among them in profile is the artist himself, who looks outside, and at the edge of the painting is a man who screams in astonishment. However, Caravaggio also paints himself next to the gravedigger as the man who looks at Christ and is partially captured by his light: an unsettling psychological implication for anxiety coupled with hope. The painter does not wish to camouflage his personal dramatic fate. He too, is Lazarus: in those days, his life hung by a silk thread and his death could take place at any moment.

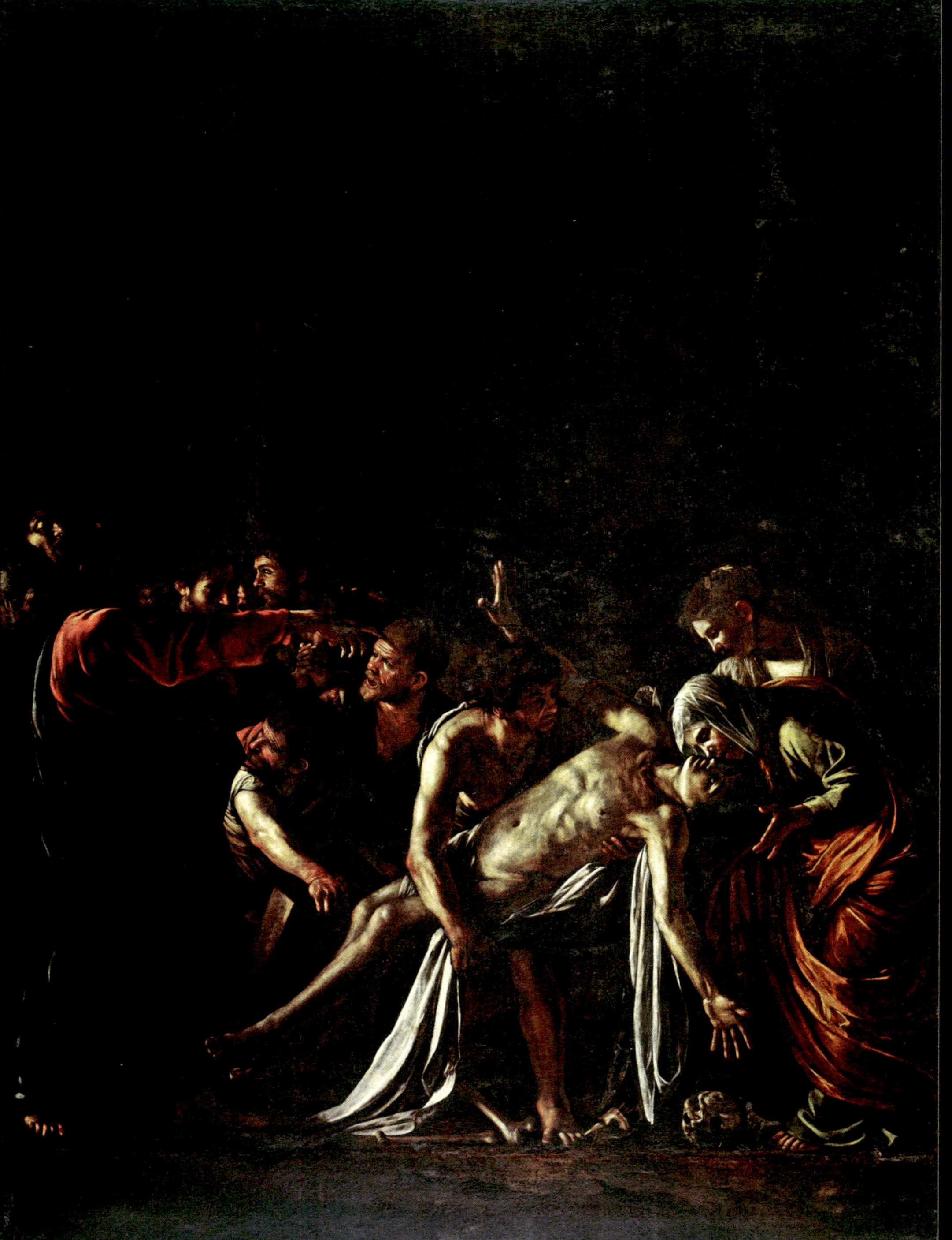

In this way, he focuses upon the dilemma of life and death, expressed in the brownish nuances of colors, in the red fields of color, which recall the theme of bloodshed, and in the dark areas, where the light struggles to penetrate, but nonetheless does so with certainty.

The gesture of the Messiah is decisive. Life can conquer death. It does for Lazarus, it will for Christ. The painter, with an anxiety which lingers throughout the entire painting, hopes the same for himself and hence, for every man.

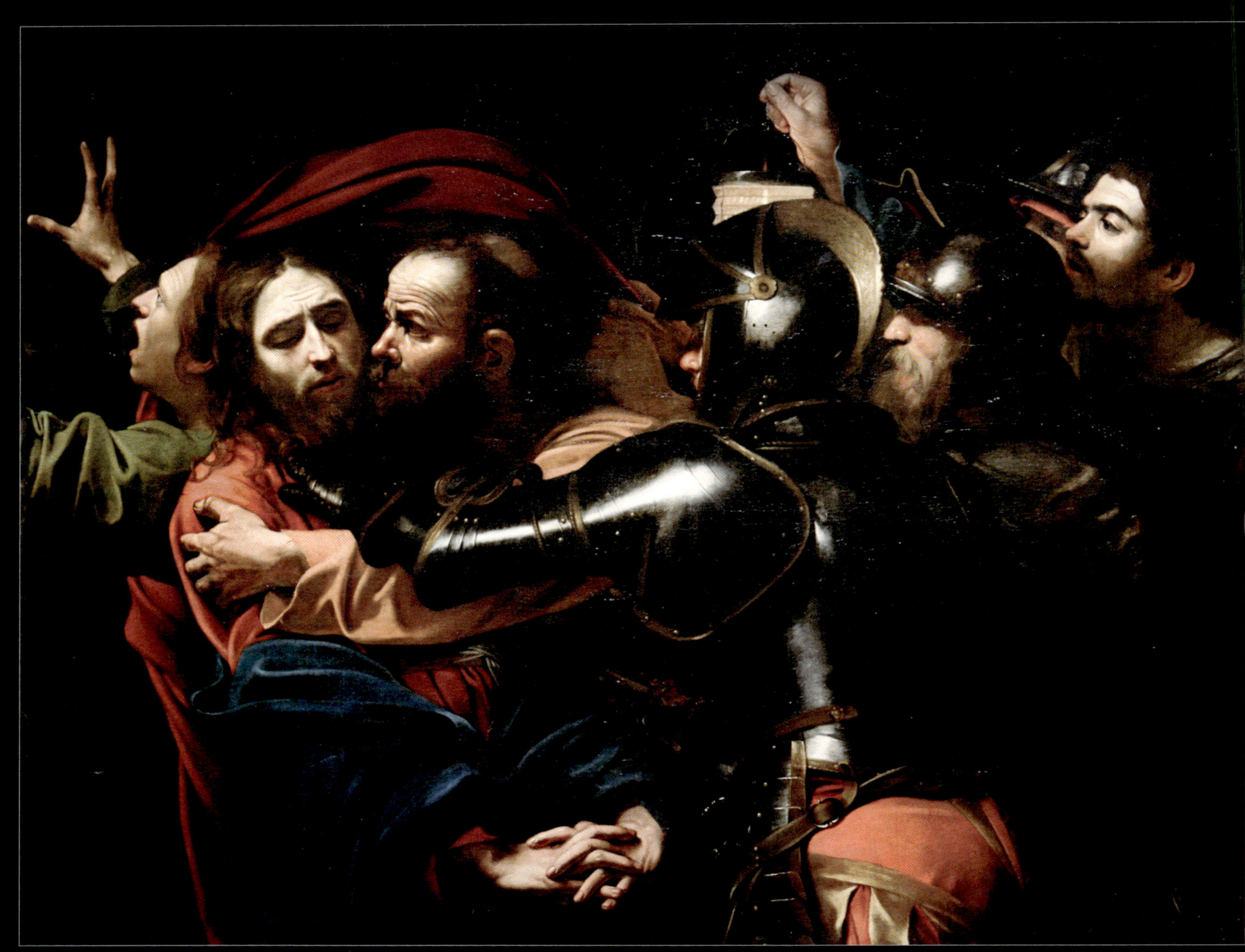

9. Taking of Christ

Oil on canvas, 133.5 x 169.5 cm. Dublin, National Gallery of Ireland.

The *Taking of Christ*, which is mentioned in all four Gospels, was painted by Caravaggio in 1602 according to the specifications of Gerolamo Mattei, the brother of the client Ciriaco, a protector of the Franciscan Order.

The spirituality of the Order placed great emphasis upon the virtues of *abnegatio* (self-denial) and *oboedientia* (obedience), as outlined in the famous text, *De imitatione Christi*. We recognize this in the posture of Christ: he is wrapped up in a red cloak as if in a niche, enduring the kiss of Judas with a suffering facial expression and clasped hands. With it, he expresses his acceptance of God's will without question. Still, Caravaggio's precise psychology articulates the Messiah's instinctive rejection of the traitor's embrace. Corresponding to the iconography steeped in tradition, culminating with Giotto's fresco for the Scrovegni Chapel, Judas is the embodiment of evil. His powerful embrace is accentuated via the yellow ocher sleeves and unattractive face. The wordless dispute between Christ and Judas becomes the fulcrum of the composition of half-figures, each one displaying its own dynamic.

In the foreground stands a soldier in an iron suit of armor upon which light is reflected; he grabs hold of the Messiah at the throat with a sweeping gesture, cutting the image into two parts. At his side, we see an older soldier, who later acts as the reference for Matthew as well as Abraham, as well as two additional figures along the edges of the painting. The screaming youth at the left of the canvas is neither the boy mentioned in the Gospel of Mark nor he who, flees naked when surprised by the guards; rather, he is probably the Evangelist himself. In this image, he is shown in the red and green of the Vatican *Entombment*, and moreover, at the height of consternation that drives him to flee into the physical and moral darkness. At the other edge of the painting, a figure – a priest? – attempts to make his way with a lamp through the nightly pandemonium. Within it, experts recognize a self-portrait of the artist at 31 years of age. This priest-Caravaggio does not in fact, have much to do with the action and was evidently inserted on account of its metaphorical significance, like a new Diogenes, in search of the light of truth with his lantern. In this case, Christ is both near and unattainable.

Between these two extremes, desperation and retrieval, the nocturnal tragedy takes place. The night is dark, the light garish; it brings the bodies, particularly the faces, closer to one another, offering a crescendo of feelings and emotions of the highest expression: from John's scream to Jesus' submissiveness, from Judas' gloom to the invisible face of the iron-clad figure, from the older soldier to the painter with the lantern, to a last, unidentifiable profile which is lost in the shadows.

Caravaggio freezes the figures, in that he sculpts them as if in relief utilizing the aggressiveness of light and color. With varying, constantly-moving sources of light, he explores the distinctive light-dark of a sudden ambush. This elevates the substance of the Gospel episode and brings it into the present: one of arrest, of conflict between the innocent and human justice, events that the artist and his audience both knew. Arising from this tumult of humanity without internal light is Christ, with his red garment (renewing the "theme of bloodshed"), the sallow face, the individually articulated strands of hair, and the lowered hands as a symbol of unconditional surrender. These, however, never detract from his dignity as an innocent man offended by the devious gesture of affection.

Following the capture of Christ in the Gospel account of the Passion is the trial of Jesus, of which the denial of Peter is a part. Caravaggio painted this in an oil on canvas (94 x 125.4 cm., New York, Metropolitan Museum of Art) between 1609 and 1610.

The image is focused upon the apostle, who guides his hands to his chest in a gesture of avowal, while the wife of a soldier points to him. The muted palette of colors, the neutral background, and the cold light make clear the regret of perjury and the fear of death. The painting captivates through the inferability of Caravaggio's exploration of human weakness and the feeling of guilt; in this manner, he even surpasses Rembrandt.

Lastly, a painting from about 1603 (154 x 122 cm.) should be mentioned, showing Christ at the beginning of the Passion in the Garden of Gethsemane, but was destroyed in Berlin in 1945. Light accentuates the outstretched body of Peter, who has been reprimanded by Jesus, and falls upon the two sleeping apostles next to him. A sharp chiaroscuro emphasizes the theatrical and emotional impression of the event.

10. Flagellation of Christ

Oil on canvas, 286 x 213 cm. Naples, Museo di Capodimonte.

This painting, which has been treated by countless art theorists, was painted in two sections (1607 and 1609) for Tommaso de Franchis and is an ideal expression of Caravaggio's late work. For it, he gleaned inspiration from Sebastiano del Piombo's corresponding work, based on a sketch by Michelangelo fifty years earlier for the Roman church of San Pietro in Montorio. Yet Caravaggio's spirit of execution and its corresponding impact are entirely different.

The arrangement of the scene is played up by the strong chiaroscuro, which creates the basis for the plasticity of the four figures and heightens their movements and emotions. The colors, all based upon browns, appear muted in a space, that – like other paintings by the master during this period – is closed off by a large, dark, empty wall. The threatening darkness, which looms overhead, burdens even the narrative and magnifies the fear of martyrdom that overcomes Jesus. A henchman pulls roughly at his hair, a second one binds him, a third one lays down the whip in preparation.

The light coils itself above the bodies, giving the event an almost frenzied dynamic and "photographs" the lightning-like speed of the torture by the three figures, who are practiced at torturing their fellow men. Caravaggio participates in the unusual pathos; he makes the Gospel story modern through clothing and gestures, so that it takes place in the here and now, while the midday light defies the darkness and symbolically makes its way through the path of human malice.

It confronts the massive body of Christ, displayed in its utter corporeality, appearing almost as a heavy laborer, with its pure while loincloth interwoven with bundles of light. The bowed head of Jesus, crushed by the physical and spiritual pain and worn down by the numerous blows, embodies his dulled suffering and further exemplifies the theme of abandonment. The three figures around him seem to suddenly appear from out of the darkness and are then swallowed up by it; they circle him impetuously, while the column in the middle appears to impassively observe the scene.

Caravaggio, greatly distanced from emotionally-laden, nearly overblown versions by his contemporaries and successors, displays here the entire power of human malice. The image conveys an outcry of suffering with an intensity to rival Shakespeare. In this manner, the flagellated man becomes an exemplum of humanity as a whole, oppressed by the burden of evil and that sees no escape, save for the light, whose luminosity is

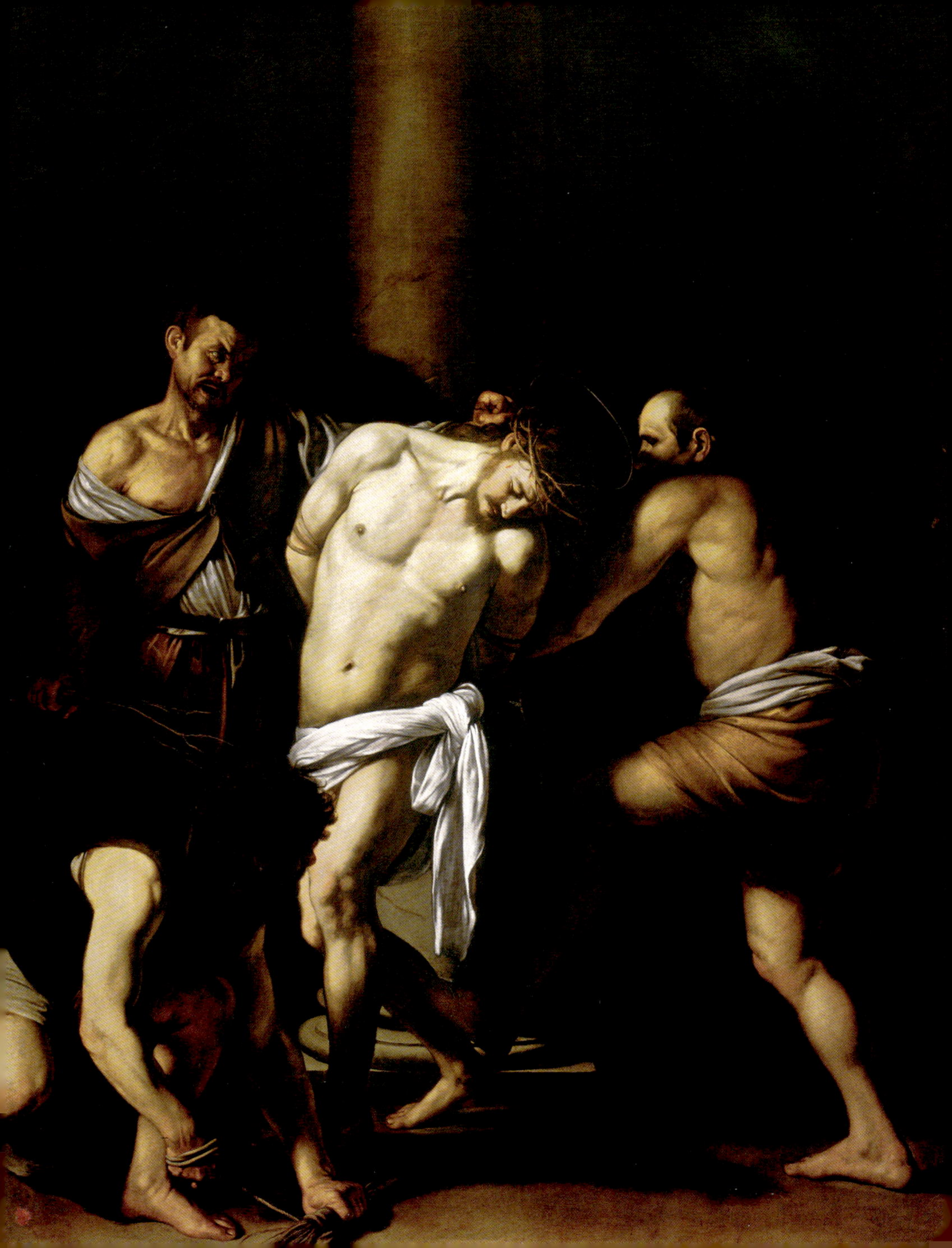

attached to Christ and which allows for a glimpse of
hope for the Messiah as well.

In 1607, Caravaggio painted another version of the
Flagellation (oil on canvas, 135.5 x 175.5 cm., Rouen,
Musée des Beaux-Arts) Three half-size (or slightly
larger) portraits in a rectangular format are shown:
two flagellants, in which the figure with the hat
resembles one of the henchmen in the Naples painting, as well as an athletic Christ who is bound to the
column. (A similar corporeality is found for reasons of
"mystical" interpretations in a number of newer films,
such as Mel Gibson's Passion of the Christ).
Caravaggio contrasts the the frenzied dynamic of the
first painting here with the terrible limbo of anticipa-
tion of the first strike of the whip. The image finds
expression in the pleading gaze, directed towards the
Heavenly Father. Abandonment, already present in
John the Baptist, again becomes thematicized, now
applying to Christ himself. With his classically muscular corporeality, which becomes nearly three-dimen-
sional by means of chiaroscuro, he leans his torso
forward, as if he wished to destroy the canvas with its
oppressive physical and spiritual darkness in order to
find an answer. The light is nearly tangible, causing the
three bodies, as well as the loincloth and blood-red
mantle upon the stool to oscillate.

The image describes the stillness before the scream, a
new angle in painting, which Caravaggio communi-
cates through the figures' various expressions: those of
the henchmen are hardened and tense; Christ, by
contrast, appears defeated. He becomes the incarcer-
ated and innocent martyred par excellence.

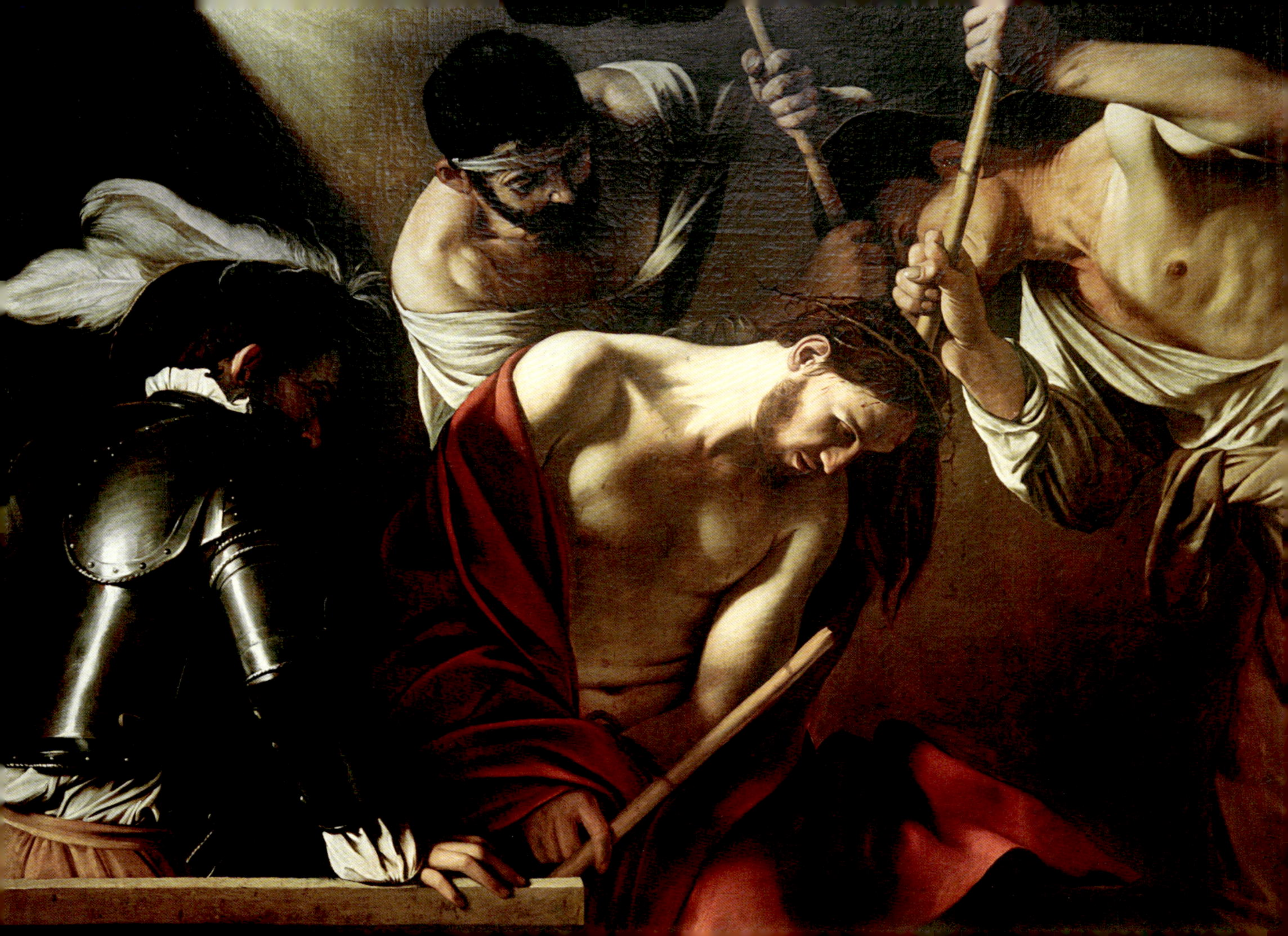

11. The Crowning with Thorns

Oil on canvas, 127 x 165.5 cm. Vienna, Kunsthistorisches Museum, Gemäldegalerie.

Included in the three Gospels by Matthew, Mark, and John, this event has been depicted in countless variations over the centuries. Caravaggio painted it in 1603 for the collector Vincenzo Giustiniani.

The artist was evidently influenced by Titian's two paintings of *The Crowning with Thorns* (now in Munich and Paris), in his emphasis upon the suffering Christ with lowered head, whose body threatens to collapse from the henchmen's blows.

The horizontal canvas displays a scene with half-portraits, whose violence is magnified by their almost wild ferocity. Caravaggio articulates the henchmen's utterly merciless torture, their rough blows upon the Christ's head nearly audible. Their faces are partially hidden by the whipping reeds, while a beam of light, like a spotlight, illuminates the scene. It conveys, as it always does with Caravaggio, a physical as well as symbolic light, specifically, God's view upon human suffering. It expands, accentuating the physical constitution of Christ, illuminating the purple robe and the two contemporarily dressed men, embodiments of raw violence. It underlines the weak and yet majestic body of the oppressed, the red, folded curtain, and the two men.

On the other hand, it is the light which divides the canvas into two sections and reflects upon the armor of the presumably Venetian soldier, who appears either indifferent or indecisive. Caravaggio allows for the play of chiaroscuro, only that here, it assumes a startling, dramatic value via the impulsive, slender brushstrokes that resemble a painting by Tintoretto.

The juxtaposition of the face of Jesus and that of the henchman is unusual, contrasting mercy and brutal barbarism. This Christ, who is about to sink exhaustedly to the ground, radiates an enormous moral strength, his mouth slightly parted in pain, while the cane nearly slips from his hand from fatigue.

Caravaggio inserts a profound, genuine pity into this representation: the Messiah is the Man of Sorrows, innocence is persecuted by the injustice of fellow man, set within the silent and numb cell like the universally imprisoned.

In this image, too, the blood red plays an important role: in the drops which flow from the head of Jesus upon his chest, in the purple robe, and in the "blood of the soul" which the mystics of the era referred to as the inner-spiritual trials of Christians and the Messiah. The redeeming function of Christ's blood is crystal clear, for he paid for the freedom of the people with his life.

As evidenced by the artist's personal sketches, Caravaggio executed an additional painting with the same motif

in 1600–1602, (oil on canvas, 178 x 125 cm., Prato, Cassa di Risparmio) for Massimo Massimi. Upon a vertical canvas, we see a bare-chested Christ, illuminated by a light entering from the left and that also reaches to the back of a young man. This displays echoes of a similar representation in the *Martyrdom of Saint Matthew* (Rome, San Luigi dei Francesi). Markedly less light are the soldier, who presses the crown of thorns onto Christ and the henchman, who restrains him firmly.
The Messiah lets out an involuntary groan, manifested by the uplifted hand and the heavenward gaze in search of comfort.

The scene exposes a dull pain, with the close juxtaposition of the torturers and the tortured elevating the tension, infusing the painting with an atmosphere of physical and spiritual oppression.
Caravaggio, who has depicted himself in the torturing solider, becomes personally involved in the sober atmosphere of the event. The raw, stocky figures stand out in a sculptural, even monumental way, as reddish-hued, sharply-illuminated, sculptured images. The work of art expresses a profound unease, a soundless drama, that is weighty and turbulent.

12. Ecce Homo

Oil on canvas, 128 x 103 cm. Genoa, Galleria Civica di Palazzo Rosso.

The contract for this painting was signed on June 25, 1605 by Massimo Massimi. Evidently he was not satisfied with Caravaggio's work, for he replaced it with a more lofty and traditional painting of the same name by Cigoli (Florence, Palazzo Pitti, Galleria Palatina) two years later.

His atypically horizontal painting was intended for personal devotion and in correlation to the standards of Venetian painting, displays three sculptural figures behind a balustrade. From out of the darkness emerge Christ, an evildoer, and Pilate; they are illuminated by a shallow light that shines brightly upon the body of a handsome, docile Christ, who concentrates upon his staunchly accepted pain. In this transcendental serenity of Christ is the echo of a mystical tradition emphasizing his absolute submission to God's will, also typical of the Biblical "servant of God," in which the Catholic exegesis recognized a prophecy of Christ's Passion. The chaotic, screaming crowd which is mentioned in the Gospels (especially in Chapter 19 of the Gospel of John) is not visible here. It is implied and only reflected – in an originally theatrical invention – in the features of Pilate, a grotesque caricature of a contemporary judge, and in the indistinct traits of the henchman, who is precisely as ugly as all of his

"colleagues" in similar paintings, for they are truly the instruments of evil.

By contrast, Caravaggio all at once bypasses the entire traditionally figurative currents, which often value emotional or sentimental aspects (Moretto, Tintoretto), the spectacular (Barocci) or the resigned pain of Jesus amidst diabolical figures (as in North European art, such as Bosch, Grünewald, or Schongauer). He develops a compositional design, in which classical influences and realistic approaches display a strongly emotive, colorful, and spiritual contrast.

In this way, the canvas becomes a display of good (Christ with his solid physique which is simultaneously realistic and idealized) and evil (Pilate's hypocrisy and the henchman's stupidity). Caravaggio articulates the thoughts of these men. In the judge, clad in black with his deafening gesture, he accentuates the eyes with the highly-arched brows, the dark face and the uncombed beard; with the henchman, who lays the scarlet curtain upon the shoulders of the Messiah, he emphasizes the parted mouth with its final taunt.

With Christ, which might even constitute a portrait, the beard was added later. The light tones of the master's color range are only applied to the loincloth.

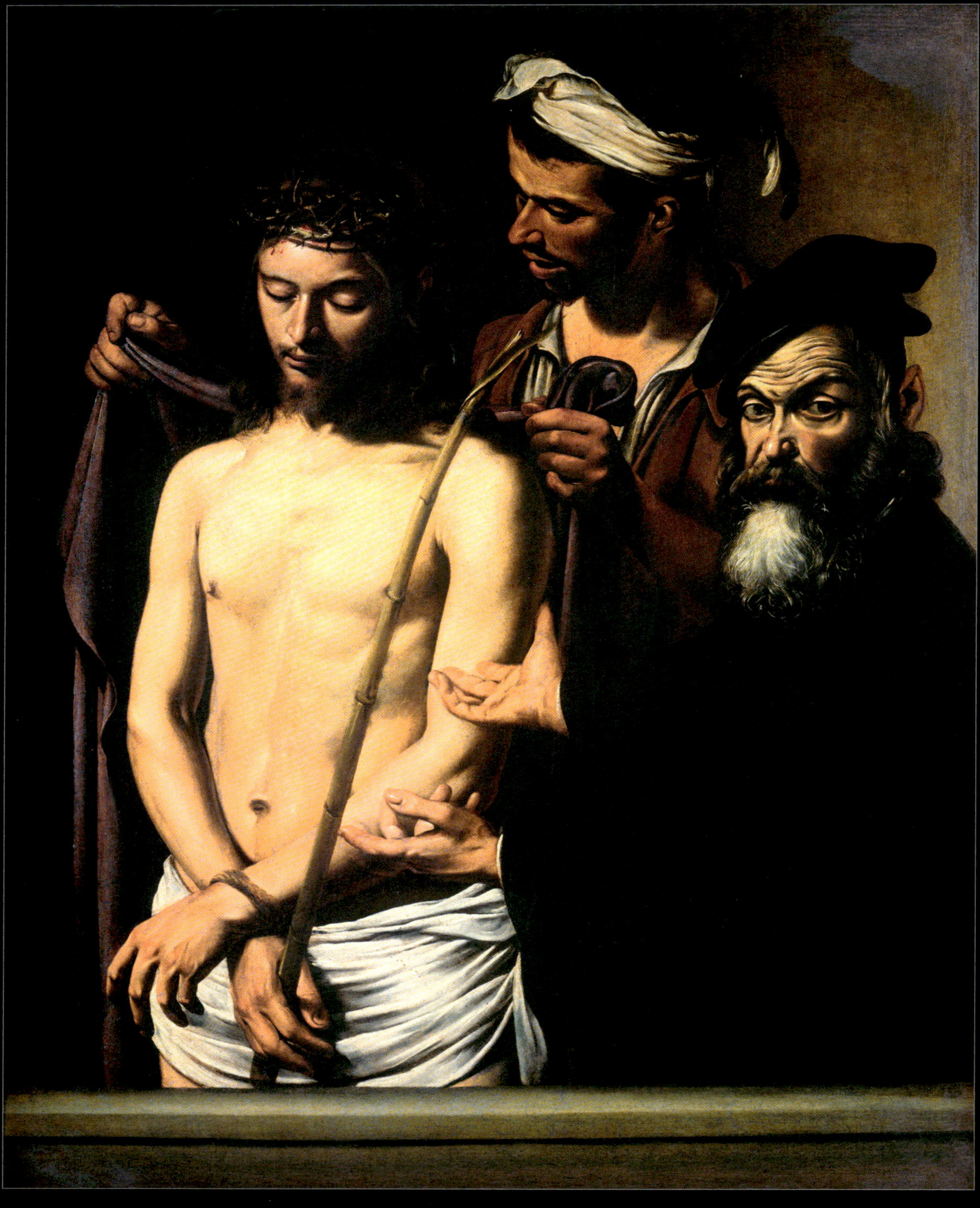

The thorn tips are hinted at with a few light flecks of paint; only a few drops of blood are made visible. We tend to remain in the sphere of contemplation rather than that of realistic description – precisely the opposite of the painting's other component, which quite deliberately mocks human justice, as if the artist himself had countless reserves of material in this regard. In fact, it involves a personal touch which exposes the artist's (arguably irate) participation. Still, even this is consistent with the overall image, for the peaceful Christ creates harmony between opposites, made possible by thick color strokes reserved for him and differing from the rapid strokes Caravaggio used to paint the other two figures.

In spite of all this, a strange sensation of peace radiates throughout the image, unusual for Caravaggio as well as for standard representations of this type. The painting goes on to inspire and become an example for numerous artists, even for the more sentimental works by Guido Reni and Guercino.

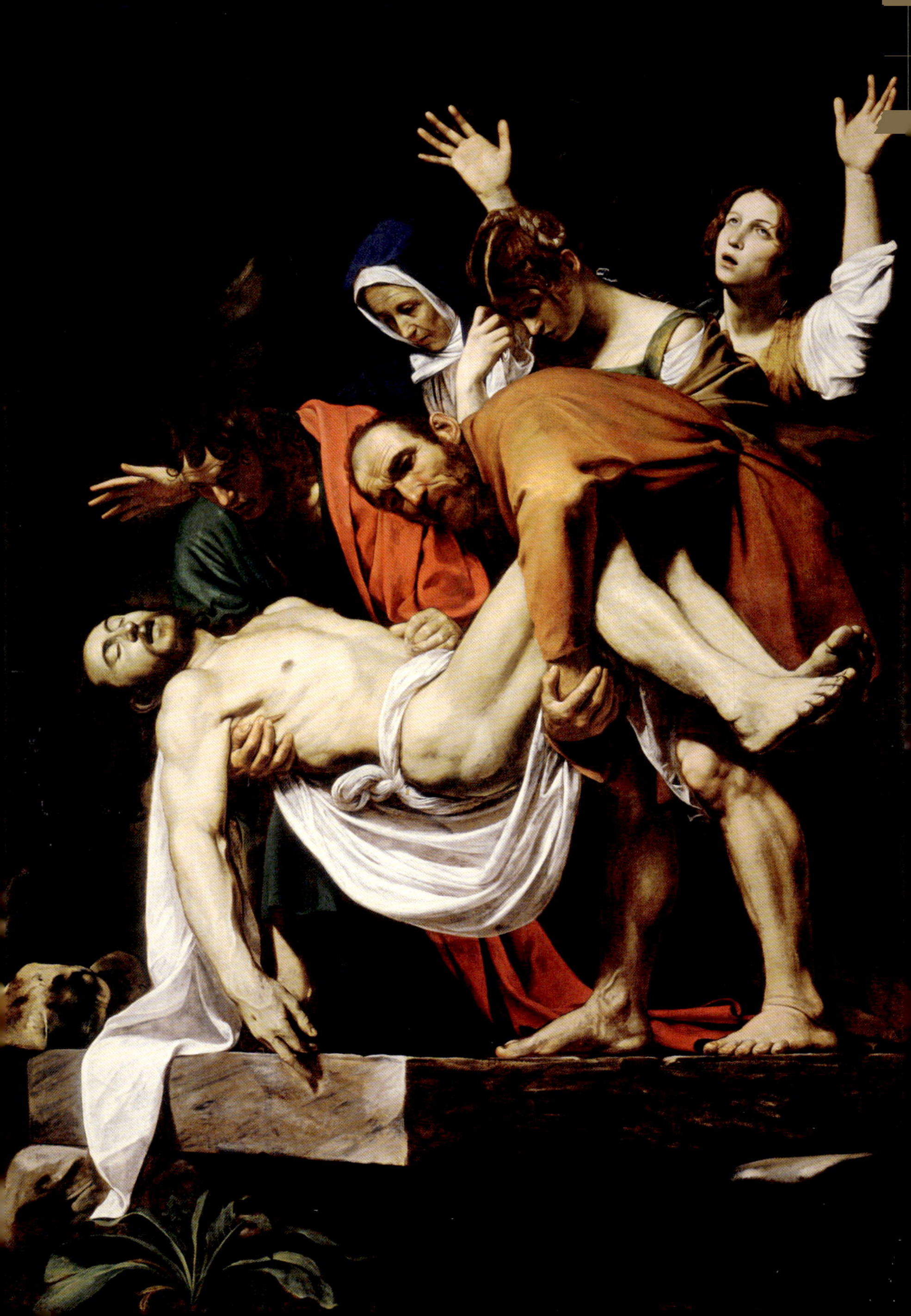

13. The Entombment of Christ

Oil on canvas, 300 x 203 cm. Rome, Pinacoteca Vaticana.

The painting was executed between 1602–1604 for the church of the Oratorians of Saint Philipp Neri, Santa Maria in Vallicella. More so than an entombment, the master presents the transport of Christ to the burial site, as was typical of Christian iconography at the time. We detect strong echoes of the work by the same name by Raphael (Rome, Galleria Borghese), for Merisi too, adopted the drooping arm of the dead Jesus from Michelangelo's *Pietà* in St. Peter. Yet he was also inspired by the famous *Entombment* by Daniele da Volterra (Rome, Trinita' dei Monti), a friend of Michelangelo.

The canvas embodies a type of "classic interlude" in the *oeuvre* of the artist, who stages a painting that is festive, theatrical, in the sense of a religious play – perhaps even with an echo of the life-sized "Compianti" sculptures of the 15th century in the Emilia region. The funeral extends to the dark cavern of the tomb (the darkness of death). It is "hewn out in the rock" (Matthew 27:60) and the large stone has already been lifted to clear the passage. The account in the four Gospels is sparse, concise, but not Caravaggio's representation of it. Its delineated eloquence is mirrored within a church, where the faithful were meant to be specifically guided through the reality of the "true death" of Christ, in a combination of impoverishment, beauty, and truth.

The body of the Messiah is vigorous, athletic, suffused with light, with the sagging head and deadly-pale face almost having the effect of a portrait. John and Nicodemus carry him to the grave, closely followed by three women. They are the Mother of God, with her noble, aged face and arms extended like a cross (illustrating the "Passion" of the Virgin Mary, who is regarded as a "co-savior" in Catholic spirituality), Mary Magdalene, who is shown weeping (corresponding to the reading as the famous penitent sinner who bathed the feet of Jesus with her tears), and Mary of Clopas, who raises her arms towards heaven in grief, an archaic gesture of funereal lamentation.

The scene is brought close to the viewer with the use of vibrant color: the red and the green of John's clothing, the blue of the Madonna's robe, the yellow and white tones of the two other women, and the orange-brown of Nicodemus (an unequivocal portrait of Michelangelo, who also depicted himself in the *Pietà* for the Florence Cathedral as Nicodemus, the "first Christian sculptor"). In keeping with the age-old request of the believer's participation in the painful lamentation, he gazes at us.

Pain is piercingly articulated, rendered both in the raised arms of Mary of Klopas and in the tearless features of the two disciples. The light upon Jesus' body and the new white loincloth appear to anticipate the Resurrection; light is the material and spiritual link between the mourners, who are all placed in their monumentality at the foreground of the image. Amidst this immense grief and despite every evidence of pain, the painter simultaneously channels a feeling of hope. Exempt from this is the mother of Jesus, for she is characteristically portrayed as the one who "safeguards everything in her heart" (Gospel of Luke), specifically, in a meditative posture that displays her suffering less overtly. However, it is expressed quite clearly in the "spiritual crucifixion" of her outreached arms. This *Entombment* was orginally not conceived as an independent work. It belonged to the configuration of the church with its 15 chapels, each meant to have a mystery of the rosary dedicated to it. As this Catholic Marian prayer achieved its final form in the 16th century, the *Entombment* was intended to be a stage of contemplation and meditation upon pain and glory.

Death becomes understood as an absurd sorrow, finding expression in the dark background, from which the figures emerge like bronze sculptures. They are seemingly propelled by a blazing light which originates beyond the pictorial frame. As in other works, this light is also a carrier of hope amidst the all-too human fear of the unfathomable reality of death, which was also endured by Christ. Yet, the stone in front of the tomb "had already been moved" as a sign of the Messiah's resurrection.

14. Supper at Emmaus

Oil on canvas, 141 x 175 cm. Milan, Pinakothek Brera.

Caravaggio painted this image (after the murder of Ranuccio Tomassoni on May 6, 1606) at an estate of the Colonna family in Paliano or Palestrina not far from Rome. It is incredible how the artist could paint such an inspired, focused work while in hiding. The mystery of the Resurrection (Luke 24) is articulated with an element of surprise, loneliness and the observation of an event, that according to the painter, can be repeated even anywhere today, even in a tavern (see *The Calling of Saint Matthew*). Distinctive is the echo of the Bible of the poor and the humble, who were dear to Caravaggio.

The horizontal composition recalls Lombard-Venetian painting (Bassano, Moretto, and Titian) and the shadowy atmosphere of Leonardo. The masculine Christ with his classic physiognomy has just broken the bread and is now blessing it. The Gospel characterizes this as the event at which the disciples identified the resurrected Master. We recognize the amazement of the farmer seated on the right from his raised eyebrows and as he grips the table with both hands. His left, overdimensional, protruding ear (a reference to the Gospel of Luke?) appears to want to listen to the words of Christ with especial attention.

The face of the other disciple remains in shadow, his posture also registering surprise. The two standing figures (inkeeper and maid) show varying reactions: he looks on questioningly and with curiosity; she (a mature female type who reappears in other paintings) lowers her gaze within a wrinkled face and looks more respectful and pensive. In the painter's opinion, they represent two different spiritual attitudes with regard to the mystery: the innkeeper questioning, the maid accepting. Caravaggio also describes these emotions using elements of light and color that have been reduced to their essentials.

On the table can be seen bread, a pitcher of wine, a plate with vegetables: the sustenance of the local people. Theatricality does not dominate the scene, which more so conveys the impression of a domestic, straightforward religious play. Christ emerges gently from the shadows, surrounded by a low, warm light which approaches from the left; it illuminates a portion of his face and the hand raised in blessing, incorporating the entire table and ultimately spreading towards the standing figures, to be lost in the shadows of the woman's breast. It leaves an imprint with the outline of a fish, an early Christian symbol signaling the presence of Christ.

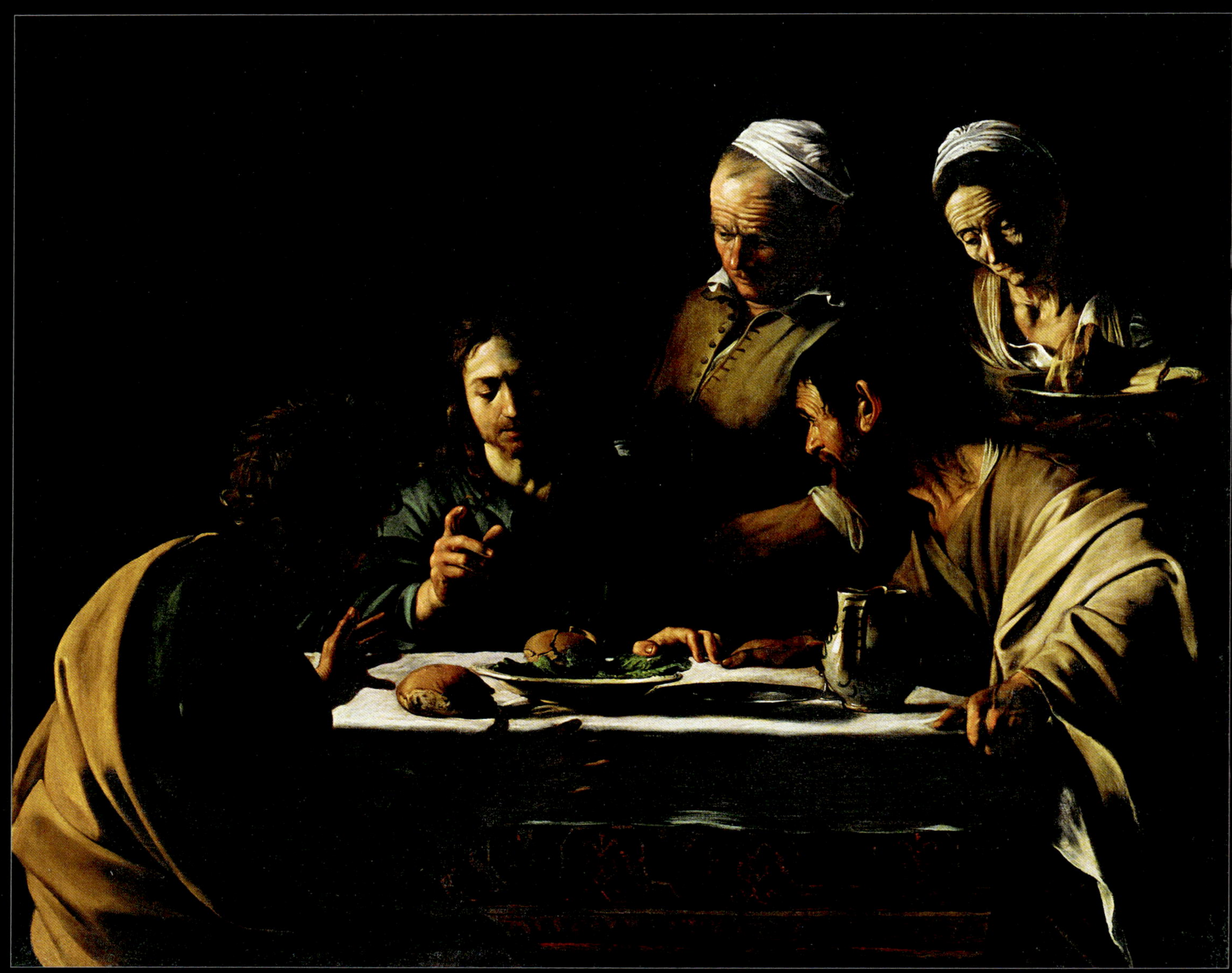

One notices the diagonal composition with its dividing line between light and dark, typical for the painter. Caravaggio generates life from out of the darkness. Yet the play of light and dark is restrained here, taken in, in a taste of Rembrandt. Caravaggio specifically does not give us the dramatic moment in which a dead man proves to be among the living and in doing so, causes shock and disturbance. Rather, he presents the wholly discreet appearance-manifestation of the divine in everyday life. The positioning of Christ's hand indicates the final benediction at the end of the Catholic Mass.

Despite or due to its great simplicity, the sacred event is imbued with a profound spiritual meaning that incorporates the figures. Christ, utterly focused upon his actions and conceivably saddened by the disciples' disbelief and his impending departure from the world, shall momentarily disappear, and only then will the disciples believe. One must not observe this painting for a long period to appreciate its charged symbolism. Restrained emotions, muted pigments, and sparse brushstrokes convey a fundamentally religious feeling. In particular, it appears to accumulate at the "empty" space at the upper left, where Caravaggio presents the concrete personality of the "mystery."

The painting of the same name, which was completed for Ciriaco Mattei in 1602 (oil on canvas, 141 x 196.2 cm., London National Gallery) is by comparison as "cinematographic" as a Tintoretto with its numerous objects, gestures, and emotions. It depicts the sudden entrance of the divine in the life of mankind. The elder disciple extends his arm out in the manner of a cross, the younger one leaps from his chair. Christ, shown beardless as in images by Michelangelo or in early Christian art that was newly-rediscovered at the time, appears refreshingly youthful in his strongly red and white robes. He blesses and at the same time consecrates the meal (as in Leonardo da Vinci's *The Last Supper*) on the richly-covered table; the bowl of out-of-season fruit (the "signature" of the painter) threatens to topple due to the disciple's uncontrolled movement. The innkeeper looks quizzically at Jesus, who stands out like a sculpture from the shadows. Truly virtuoso radiant effects are evident ranging from the still life of the wine carafe, to the clothing (note the tear in the jacket above the elbow), to the carpet on the table. It is a resurrection with a thoroughly positive character, the triumph of life over death. Caravaggio, the painter of life, feels this with the greatest intensity, and from it results a theatricality of emotions, of color, of light.

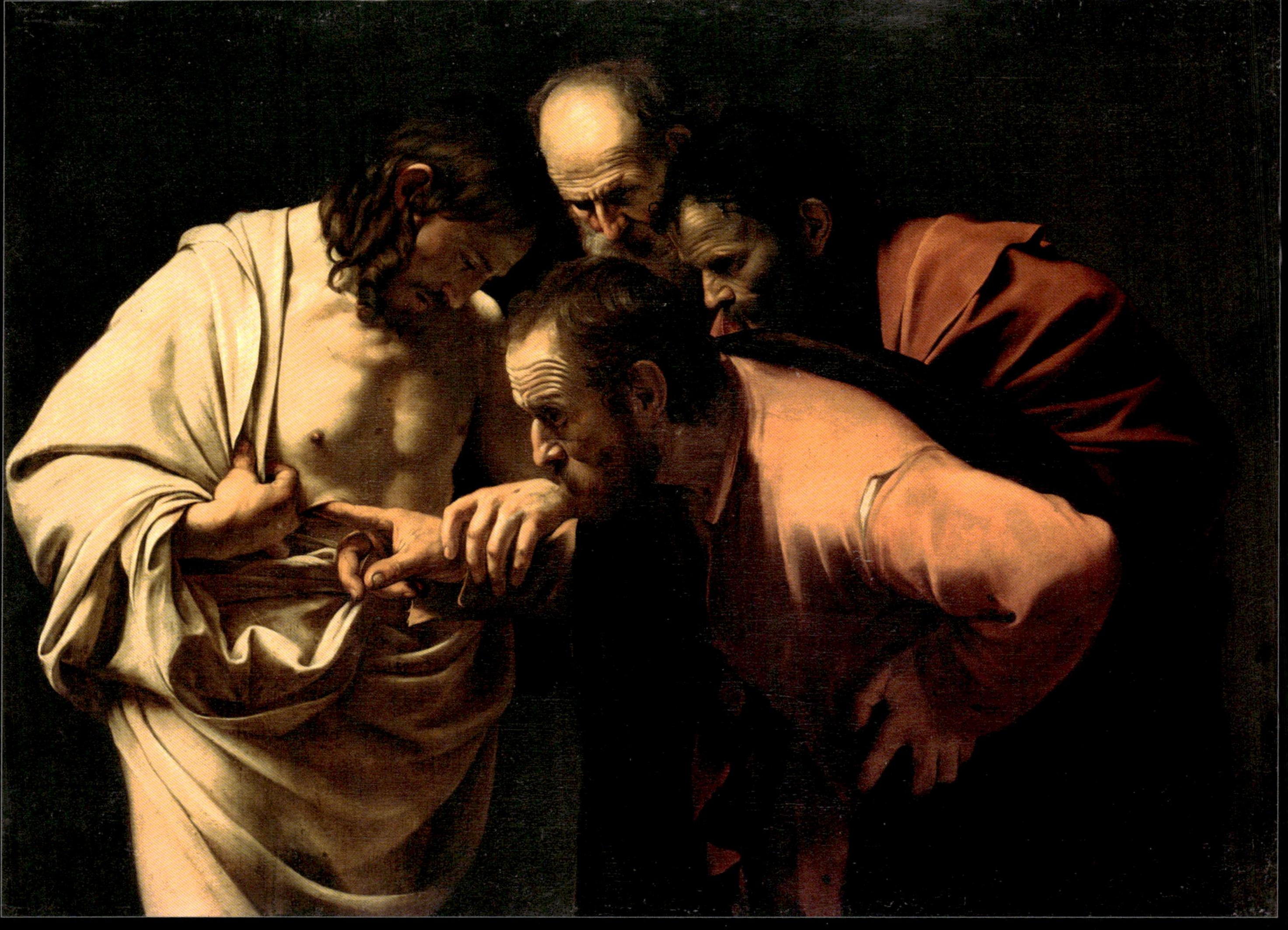

15. The Incredulity of Saint Thomas

Oil on canvas, 107 x 146 cm. Postdam-Sanssouci, Bildergalerie.

The painting, formerly part of the collection of Margrave Vincenzo Giustiniani, dates back to 1600–1601, as Caravaggio began to establish a name for himself in Italy and throughout all of Europe. The artist takes up the theme of "believing for the sake of belief" (John 20) and the need of the non-believer to be able to grasp the divine, which gained decisive importance during the period of Catholic reform. He solved the problem in his own way, without ostentation, as Sebastiano del Piombo and Dürer had done. The horizontal canvas provides the subsurface for four half-portraits in the Venetian style, similar to a movie closeup.

As Caravaggio's first Christological subject, it holds an elevated art historical and stylistic significance with regard to the master's development. Yet it reveals a (perhaps not even involuntary) parallel between the Passion of Christ and the Passion of the individual Michelangelo Merisi.

The neutral background presumably symbolizes the night of doubt and/or the spiritual darkness which overcame the disciples after the death of their master. At the front, we see the group of four, whose gaze converges upon the wound in Jesus' side. This is wrapped in a light-colored linen cloth and surrounded by a penetrating light. From the left side, the light "warms" the saturated red and brown tones of the disciples' clothing and their coarse faces, sketched from life drawings and fully focused upon seeing and touching in order to believe.

Caravaggio embodies the human quest for belief in the most natural way possible. His Christ – wrapped in a cloth according to the classic style and as a result, both residing within and outside time – demonstrates sympathy for the human struggle in his path towards truth.

Thomas, shown from the front, palpates the wound, even plunging his finger into it with the same brutal realism that the painter already demonstrated in his *Judith*. The other two "probe" it with their minds, so fully focused are they upon it. In them, Caravaggio observes the strong instinct of common sense within the human spirit.

Christ gently pulls Thomas' hand to his side, that is to say, he helps the man to discover the truth. His face is utterly human, poignant, almost as if he were reliving the pain of the Crucifixion on account of the disciple's unbelief. It is worth noting, that Caravaggio mainly dwells upon the painful hours of the life of the Messiah and in doing so, he displays enormous sympathy with human weakness as well as with the pain that men have inflicted upon Christ.

Yet the artist is also familiar with doubt and represents it, for the Gospels frequently speak of people in despair. The monumentality of the figures seems to want to disseminate this feeling to the extreme – until the answer of the resurrected Christ, who shines as brightly as the truth.

Upon closer inspection of the painting (which is often copied, attesting to its level of popularity), the four closely united heads convey a unique network of feeling, compressed by the artist into a lavish application of color with circularly executed brushstrokes, so as to give the viewer himself the illusion before his eyes.

Saintly and human stories – as is so often the case with Caravaggio – coincide here as well. He becomes more and more engrossed in the study of human sensibility, and he even succeeds in visually capturing the emotions of the resurrected. While this may remain contained within a metaphysical sphere, it nonetheless approaches a near-human dimension.

16. Conversion On the Way to Damascus

Oil on canvas, 230 x 175 cm. Rome, Santa Maria del Popolo.

This is the second horizontal painting for the Cerasi Chapel (1600–1601). The event (always a popular subject for artists) is mentioned in the Acts of the Apostles as well as by Paul himself. It draws comparison to the fresco in the Pauline Chapel by Michelangelo, although he chose an entirely different compositional approach. In fact, the two paintings are only similar in displaying the fall from the horse and the face illuminated by light.

Michelangelo opted for an epic depiction: Christ emerges energetically from the heavens in the manner of Zeus; within an immense space, a group of figures, suspended in their gestures and expressions, observes the "conversion" of the blinded apostle.

By contrast, Caravaggio adheres strictly to the details of the Holy Scripture, giving them an intimate, not-public dimension. Aside from Saul, only a horse and a stable hand are visible and it is not known whether the scene takes place on the street or – more likely – within a room. The background is dark and only illuminated by a few moonbeams from the upper right; they break through the darkness, descend upon the back of the imposing horse to reach Saul, who has tumbled to the ground. Stillness and loneliness prevail, further accentuated by the painter via his subtle psychological insight into the image, in recounting what occurs within the spirit of the "converted." Indeed, what we observe here is more a calling than the conversion which takes place immediately afterward. Christ cannot be seen, yet the light becomes his word and image.

Paul, a young horseman, lies on the ground, his arms extended. It is a gesture of surrender to the appearance of mercy, of surprise, and of instantaneous bewilderment: three differing emotions, which are incorporated into a single scene by means of the artist's exceptional artistic imagination.

It is night. Light rays arrive not only from the light of the merciful Christ, but from the visible rays of the moon, whose weak, unobtrusive luminosity shines upon the male body. His mouth is open; he is listening. The eyes, by contrast, are closed on account of the intense brilliance, almost as if Christ himself, within the light, had struck him. In this way, the painter analyzes the physical as well as the spiritual blindness of man in the face of the unexpected that surpasses him. The warm colors are rich with wonderful harmonizing effects: from the white and brown of the massive horse – an actual scene and a true dramaturgical stroke of genius – to the face of the old stable hand, to

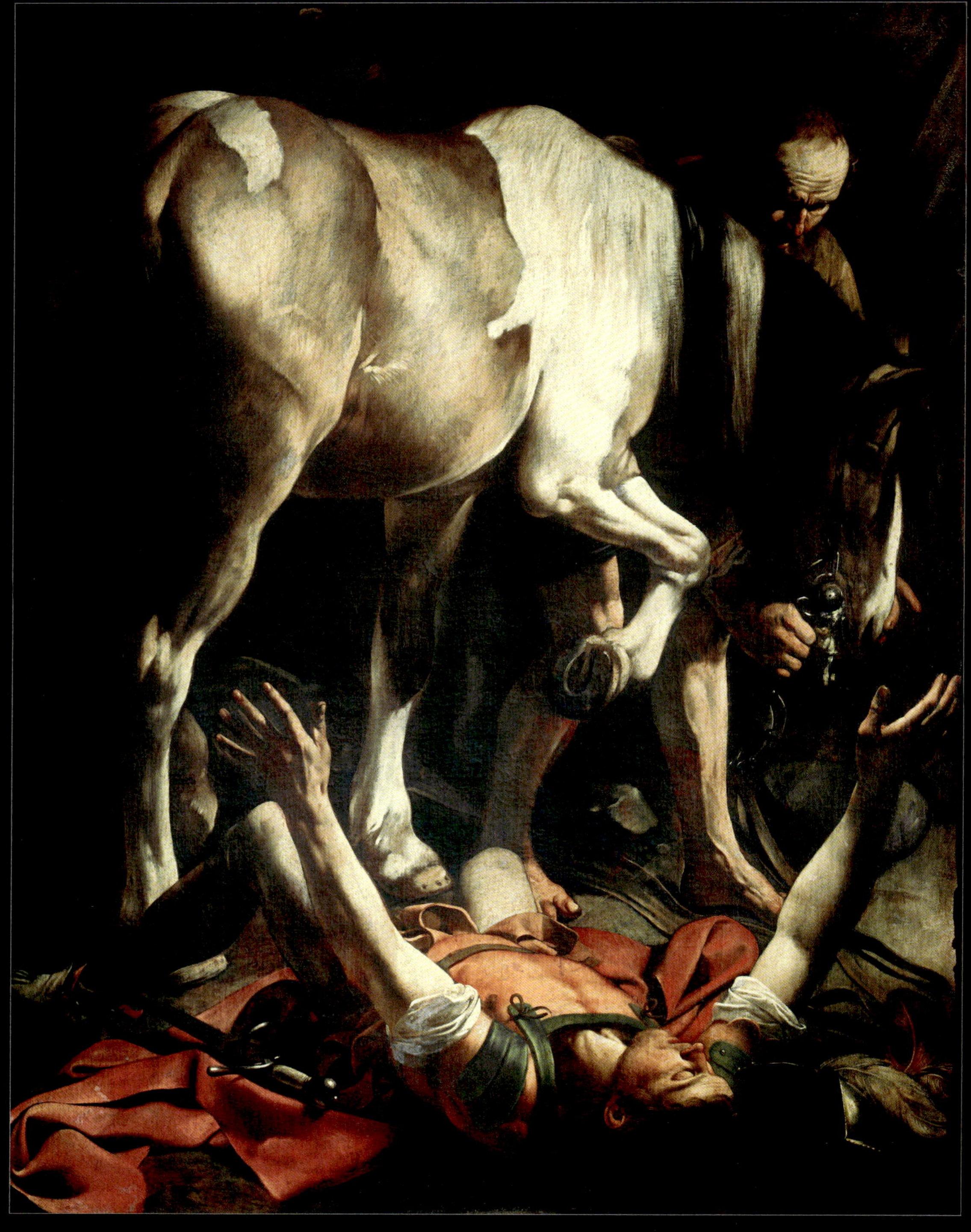

the strong red, which turns nearly pink upon the
armor, to the short, translucent-white sleeves as a
"receptacle of light"which are typical of Caravaggio.
In this still, nightly, wholly internalized painting, the
theme of conversion gains another dimension than
that in *The Calling of Saint Matthew*. There, the
equally sudden calling takes place in a public, daytime
setting. Here, it becomes a spiritual experience only
recognized by the converted. As a result, the isolation,
emphasized by the soft chiaroscuro, comes about from
the extraneous circumstances and from Saul himself.
Caravaggio's former physical naturalism is transformed into a spiritual occurrence.
Before this version, the painter had completed another one a short time earlier (oil on cypress, 237 x 189
cm., Rome, Odescalchi Collection). It was rejected,
not from the client Cerasi, who had already died, but
from his sole heir, Ospedale della Consolazione.
For this painting, Caravaggio devised a scene full of
individuals and situations. As with Michelangelo,

Christ, supported by an angel, approaches Saul from
the heavens; Saul shields his eyes from the light and is
unsuccessfully defended by a bearded warrior. We see
a sallow landscape, leaf-covered branches, a nervous
horse. The colors are unnatural, and we still perceive
the influences of the Mannerists in this exaggerated
performance, in which the cold light wanders about
freakishly. It is evident that Caravaggio was experienc-
ing a crisis of expression and he had not yet found the
sublimation that marked the final version.
In any event, the painting in its spectacularity emphasizes the topic of calling, most notably revealing its
painful aspects to us, with the contrast between the
soldier (the power of evil?), who attempts to defend
Saul from the "aggression" of Christ, and Saul, whose
rapid gesture of bringing his hands to his face also
contributes to the overheated dynamic of the painting. In this, Caravaggio unites its diverse elements
through the nearly violent flash of chiaroscuro, which
manifests the expression of a unique event.

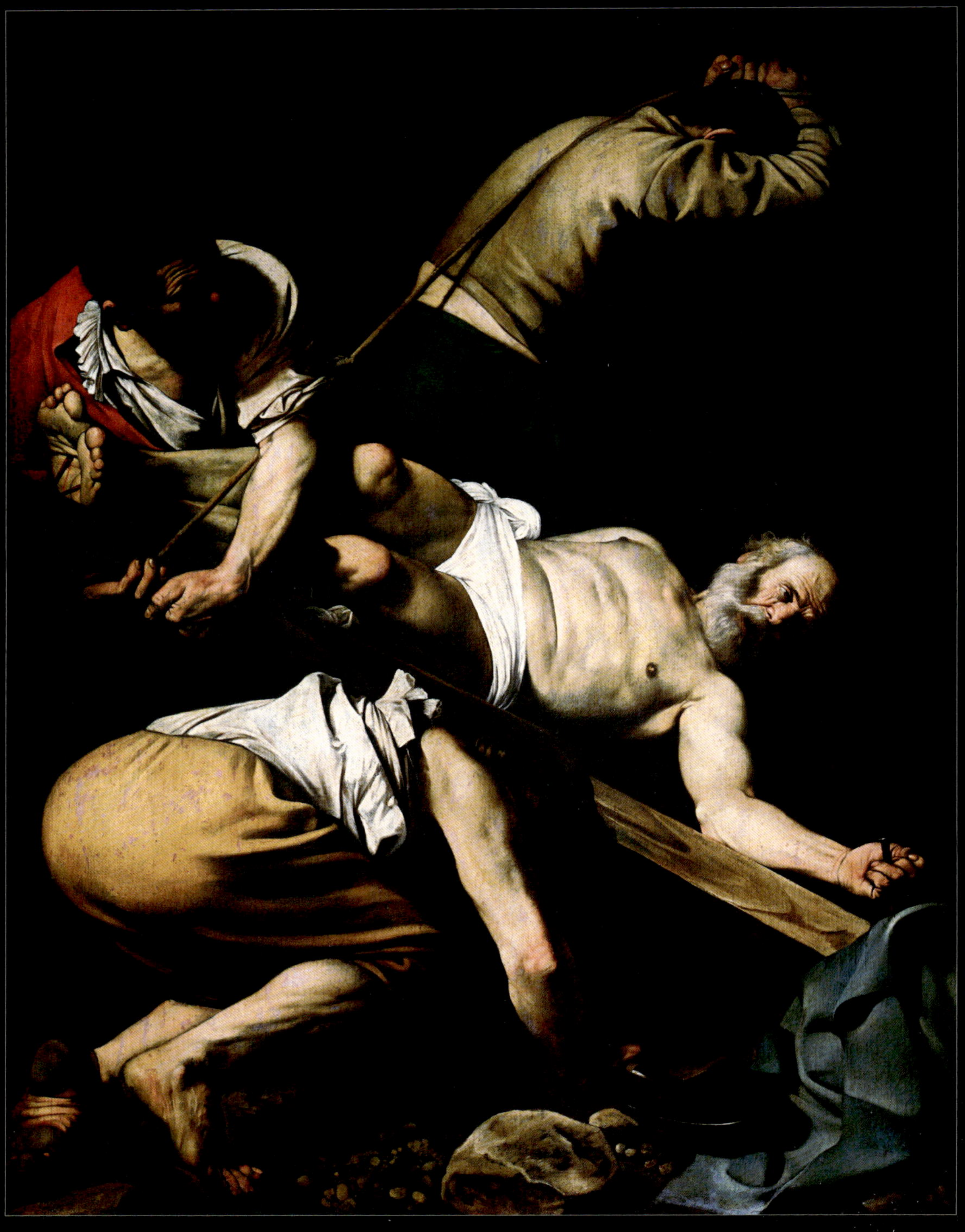

17. Crucifixion of Saint Peter

Oil on canvas, 230 x 175 cm. Rome, Santa Maria del Popolo.

The painting was executed in 1600–1601 for the Cerasi Chapel, directly following the portrayal of Saint Matthew for San Luigi dei Francesi, even as its spiritual sequel of sorts. The subject originates from the 21st chapter of the Gospel of John as well as from ancient Christian legends.

Here too, Caravaggio departs in a different direction, not portraying – as others do – the crucifixion which has already taken place, but depicting the raising of the cross. In this way, the image resembles the painting of the same name by Michelangelo in the Pauline Chapel, but without its surreal mood and abundance of figures.

The painter restricts his image to four figures: three workers and Peter. The henchmen are impressively realistic. With their tanned features and dirty feet, in their threadbare clothing, worn-out pants and torn jackets, they appear more as weary workers accustomed to hard labor than evildoers. They are a modern portrait of human labor and the lower class, who must work hard upon the brown, indented rocks.

In contrast to other depictions, we see no evil here. The saint is an old man, yet sturdily built, whose clear gaze – in spite of his physical suffering, expressed by a quick prayer – is directed at a point beyond the canvas: towards heaven, painted in an altarpiece by Annibale Carracci (*Assumption of the Virgin*) in hopes of entry.

Pain, prayer, and his acceptance of to martyrdom are evident in the countenance of the old man. A shallow light from the upper left flows around him, spreading throughout upon the neutral background and creating wonderful color combinations between white (the loincloth of the saint and the shirt of the henchman kneeling beneath the base of the cross), yellow ocher, and red (the curtain at the left). Realism of life and realism of the soul coalesce so as to stir an urgent feeling in the viewer, a feeling which appears to "capture" him, for the stillness, in which the crucifixion takes place, the rapid action, and the acknowledgment of imminent death within the faith is also manifested in the image.

Caravaggio employs light in order to compress the narrative and to focus attention upon a number of individuals, so that light becomes a "speaking" presence; so too, are the nameless bodies which provide the painter with a voice and with life. With Caravaggio, the anonymous people are in fact transformed into the protagonists of the painting. Peter is an excellent example of this: an old man as seen by many in everyday life, whom the artist converts into an allegory of power and courage of his Christian proof – as seen from the cramped, nailed-upon hand that tolerates pain to the extreme.

The painting had many imitators (such as Caravaggio's contemporary Guido Reni – Vatican Museum) and demonstrates the artist's additional step of using shadow as a form of expression. From this, the figures mature; they leap out at the viewer, becoming monumental. In doing so, they express even more convincingly Caravaggio's dramatic and symbolic concept in connection to religious themes.

18. The Death of the Virgin

The lawyer Laerzo Cherubini, a friend of Caravaggio's patron Cardinal Del Monte, had this large painting completed for his funerary chapel in the Roman church Santa Maria della Scala. It was initially hung over the altar, but then rejected by the Carmelites. Reubens purchased it in 1607 for the Duke of Mantua, Vinzent I of Gonzaga. Upon observing the highly dramatic staging for which this subject had no historical precedent, the reason for its rejection is clear. The *Dormitorio Virginis* was typically displayed in a celebratory manner or as a gentle drift into sleep (see for example, Cavallini's mosaic in Santa Maria in Trastavere).

By contrast, Caravaggio focuses the silent mourning of the poor on the death of the Mother of God with a density that approaches Shakespeare. The painter's revolution in sacred art consists of his introduction of normal people and their everyday lives in order to make the narrative more authentic.

The light creeps up onto the high, bare wall, which gradually illuminates the figures outlined in shadow. The large, blood-red curtain at the upper edge of the painting serves as a backdrop for the group of mourners. The light creates very beautiful, naturalistic effects full of meaning, in that the light grazes over the bare head of the apostle, plays upon the body of the Madonna with warm colors, to then slip over the back of the masterfully articulated, weeping Mary Magdalene, down to the gilded copper vessel. Eye-catching details are gently delineated: the hand of the Madonna, which hangs limply from the cushion, the apostle, who wipes his eyes, the closely grouped apostle heads, all expressions of muted pain, and John, lost in thought, who supports his head with his arms. Still, colors play a role: the strong red of the Virgin Mary, the yellow curtain, the white linen sheet.

Caravaggio relates pain and death as an unspeakable (one is tempted to say, inconsolable) worry in reference to the swollen body of the dead Mother of God (the distended abdomen alludes to her motherhood). This realism – but also the inability to fathom the symbolic details of the image – created scandal.

In reality, the truthfulness of the scene and the predominating feeling of sorrow achieve a thoroughly pious atmosphere, which is rare in other works deemed "religious." It is as if all of humanity wanted to mourn this death. Caravaggio is a participant in this (he is seen in profile with a yellow robe directly behind the old apostle); he imbues the painting with genuine emotion, underlined by the portrayal of an

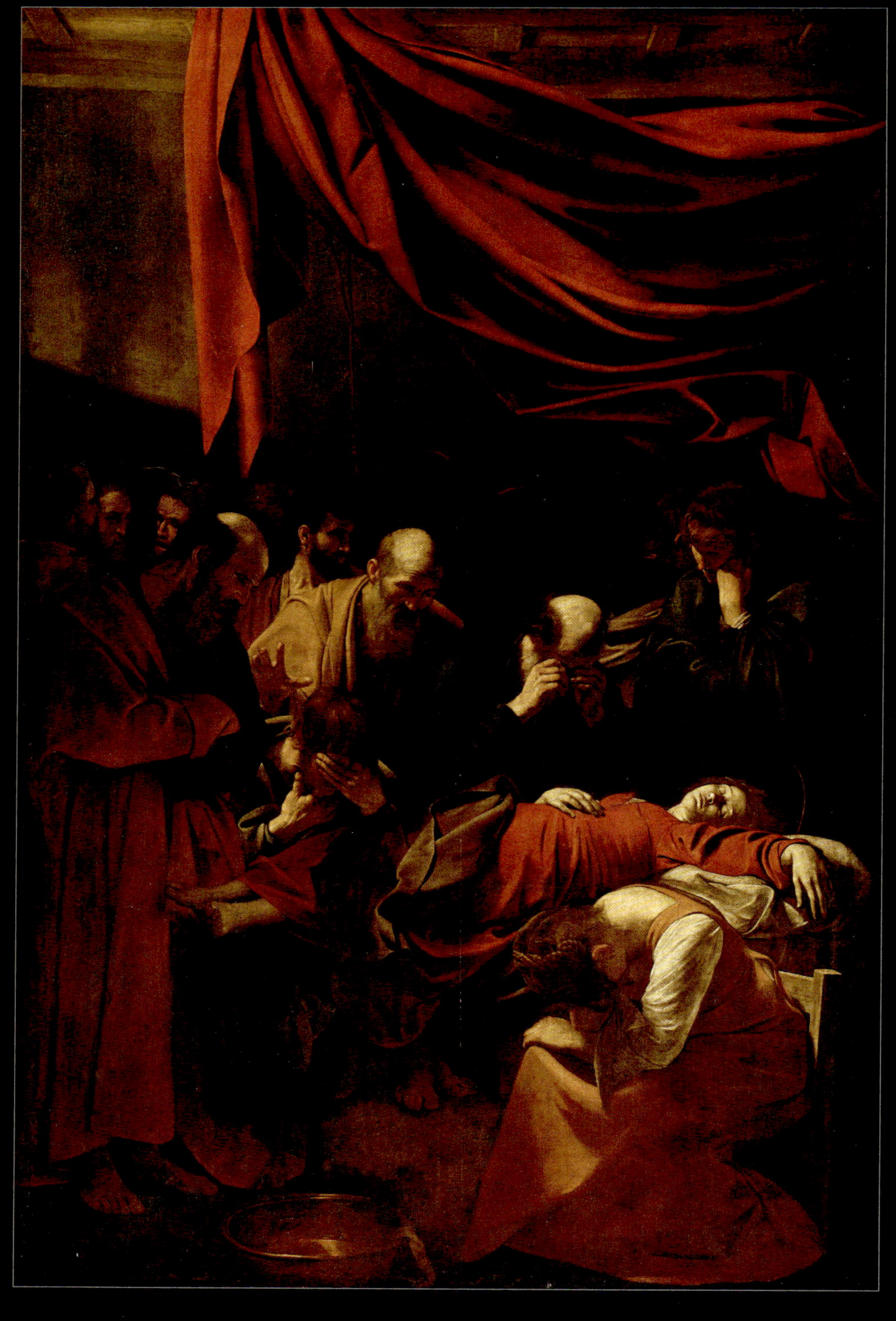

impoverished, humble setting and partially incompleted figures, as well as the few objects in the room. Death has already entered and the light displays it in both its harshness and its peacefulness. A feeling of desolation permeates the image and leaves us frozen in its bitterness, for Caravaggio wishes to bring even the deepest thoughts of each individual to the canvas. Contrast is created by the peaceful expression upon the ageless countenance of the Virgin (a reference to her "immaculateness"), who is stretched out upon her small iron bed.

The painter enables us to witness that life has abated and how difficult this reality is for man. At the Virgin's side, the pensive John (who according to the Gospel, was entrusted to remove Christ from the cross) still meditates upon the hope of perpetual life. Thus, this subject, particularly in the art of the Eastern Church, is often portrayed as the ascension of the Virgin Mary into heaven.

With this painting, Caravaggio's Biblical cycle comes to a close. Although the scene is present throughout church tradition and popular piety, it is not described in the four canonical Gospels. Still, it appears as a suitable conclusion to Caravaggio's Gospel narratives, not only on account of Mary's inclusion in the first Christian community in Jerusalem, but based upon the artist's method of representation reserved for her: a woman of his (and our) time, close to the simple folk, with whom she shares her suffering and hope.

Caravaggio's Influence on Italian and European Art

At the beginning of the 17th century, Karel von Mander from West Flanders wrote in his *Schilder-Boeck* (sketchbook) of a Michelangelo da Caravaggio, "die te Room wonderlijcke dinghen doet." Copies and original works by the artist, who was still alive, surfaced abroad, thus justifying the glory of his revolutionary style.

Although he never had his own apprentices or resourceful assistants, as was the case with the schools of Carracci or Reubens, his influence was already immense during his lifetime. It must also be kept in mind that his adventurous life, his trips to Genoa, to the Marche, to Naples, Sicily, and Malta, and his sojourns near Rome significantly reduced the possibilities of routine work.

Despite strong criticism from influential individuals such as Zuccari and Baglione, his painting style introduced a tide – partly subliminal and partly conspicuous – which pervaded throughout Europe. Many non-Italian artists were formatively shaped by him, either through prints or copies of his works or during their own stays in Italy, so that "Caravaggism" becomes characterized as an independent artistic genre of the entire 17th century and beyond.

Of course, artists enjoyed contact with Caravaggio only for a certain period of time (some more, some less), with few exceptions such as Bartolomeo Manfredi, whose *oeuvre* closely relied upon that of Michelangelo Merisi. When looking at his *Taking of Christ* (Milan, Koelliker Collection), its closeness to Caravaggio's painting is immediately discernible. Indeed, the master's art with religious subjects – that is, the topic of this volume, if not exclusively (for one must only recall the paintings with cheats, bars, gypsies, concerts, etc. which repeat and magnify Caravaggesque elements) had the greatest influence upon all of Europe. He created a type of painting whose frequently exaggerated chiaroscuro, pauper-like models, and still lifes became a common art historical language, although each artist gave it his own touch. In Italy for example, Guido Reni stood under the influence of Caravaggio before deciding to move on to Classicism. His *Crucifixion of Saint Peter* (Vatican Museum) recalls Merisi's example with respect to the young man in the feathered cap and the commonly-stylized henchmen; however, the chiaroscuro is softer and its emotions are more restrained.

Hence, Reni cautiously tried to approach Caravaggio. This was not the case with Orazio Gentileschi, whose *David and Goliath* (Dublin, National Gallery)is just as brutal and energetic as the master's image: Artemisia Gentileschi, his daughter, also paints a Judith which is even more gruesome than Caravaggio's. Additional artists, such as Guercino, who melodiously lightened the Caravaggesque shadows, or Bernardo Strozzi with his lively verismo – adopt only singular elements, and then to a lesser degree, of the aggressive art of the Lombard master.

Throughout the entire 17th century, Naples remained the center of Caravaggism. Painters such as Giovanni Battista Caracciolo (called Battistello) or the Spaniard Jusepe de Ribera (called Spagnoletto) adored light-rich contrasts, boyish youths in white robes or common folk and beggars dressed as saints, such as in Ribera's *Apostle* (Florence, Fondazione Longhi). Thus a Caravaggesque tradition took root, continuing to flourish with talented artists such as Mattia Preti and Luca Giordano.

The Frenchmen Simon Vouet, Valentin de Boulogne, and Georges de la Tour (*St. Joseph*, Paris, Louvre) recall Caravaggio's strong contrasts of light and dramatic effects; they too, revisited his subjects (such as *The Beheading of John the Baptist*). However, it was the Le Nain brothers (who had never been in Italy) who specifically embraced the teachings of the Lombard master. Their *Supper at Emmaus* (Paris, Louvre) is a feast of dignified poverty, attended by an equally needy Christ. The Le Nains adopt Caravaggio's "spirit" and his love for people, who retain their dignity even in suffering and misery. They are less interested in the spectacular light effects which attracted numerous imitators.

In an era of strong efforts against the Reformation, the Spaniards recognized the potential for religious instruction in Caravaggio's dramatics. While the "ugly" was emphasized by Ribera, Francisco de Zurbarán adhered to the mystical dimension that is present in Caravaggio's Passion imagery. Moreover, Francesco Ribalta's painting, *Christ Appears to Saint Bernard* (Madrid, Prado Museum) featuring a Messiah who emerges from the shadows and embraces the saint with an emotional gesture – with a white cloth upon white skin – is an original, already Baroque reflection of a Caravaggesque sensitivity. This holds even more true for the early works of Velasquez, who traveled to Italy on two occasions. Especially distinctive is Caravaggio's influence upon Flanders and Holland. Various masters resided for extended periods in Italy: Reubens painted the *Death of the Virgin* for the Duke of Mantua and was inspired by Caravaggio, with regard to his love of nature and theatricality of holy scenes. During his stay in Rome, Gerrit van Honthorst was strongly shaped by him and had embraced his approach. His *Christ Before the High Priest* possesses the captivating steadfastness of Merisi's works, with a naturalistic as well as symbolic light.

However, particularly evident is Michelangelo Merisi's influence on some of Rembrandt's art, who – in spite of his uncontested originality – further develops the teachings of the master. In observing the *Meal at Emmaus*, the viewer returns to the same mood of Caravaggio's painting of the same name (Milan, Pinacoteca di Brera), with a greater depth and intensity. In fact, Rembrandt completely penetrated the Christocentric spirituality of the Italian artist, with an autonomous, expressive emphasis upon the Jewish origins of Jesus.

Inventing the Truth

At the conclusion of our inquiry, this succinct phrase might define the unique style and impetus of Caravaggio's artistic activity and his exegesis of the Biblical story. Although he was regarded as a lapsed Catholic, he was actually a profound believer. However, his faith is not a naive belief in miracles, nor is he fond of a triumphant religion.

In keeping with the Catholic reforms influenced by the Council of Trent, the painter leans towards a truthful, simple view, shaped not least of all by his Lombard heritage.

Most of all and as already suggested, it seems that he was genuinely interested in the the truth. For him, the depicted events are literally an illumination of the human path towards truth. He himself also finds himself so entrenched within it, that it justifies the comparison between Christ's Passion and the personal Passion, for the Passion of the Messiah is understood and shaped through the artist's own suffering. Caravaggio highly prioritizes human dignity – and to him, Christ is truly man – which applies equally to the simple folk as it does to significant Biblical events. Sacred and human stories become one. In "inventing" his truth, the artist's task consists of making it accessible to the viewer and the faithful (one may never forget that the master's religious paintings were intended for public or private devotion) and in a manner that can be imagined today, or better yet, in a manner that can actually take place today.

One of Caravaggio's main characteristics is the conveyance of the Bible into the present. For this reason, he places the figures in familiar surroundings, observes their emotions and body language, and analyzes their naturalness as well as the authenticity of their reactions. Yet their realism is in no way a copy of the event, but rather a reconfiguration of reality, so that the newly invented truth may surface in its essentiality and universality. Caravaggio stages the life of Christ and the Biblical narrative in the manner of a religious play that arouses emotions and feelings and is intended to inspire meditation. He cites the masters from the past and the present, even challenges them, in developing a language of art that retains the old, yet bravely and powerfully opens up to the new.

Color and light, but above all, shade, are employed in a strongly appealing, for it is indeed human, art. This explains to us why his approach seems so modern – no pauper-like art or simply exaggerated realism, but rather an exciting interpretation of reality. Yet physicality and blood, pain and the little happiness of his short career do not lead to a dismal outcome. Although he is certainly familiar with long nights of the soul, through which he (like only a few of his colleagues) can penetrate into the Biblical subjects, having experienced them to some extent himself, Caravaggio safeguards his trust in life and his zest for life until the end, up until his last, nearly desperate paintings. In so doing, he remains human until the end – like Christ, with whom Caravaggio concerned himself most intensely.

In the entire history of art, few other works contain as many revolutionary elements as Caravaggio's Bible. It is deeply human and as a result, profoundly spiritual as well. For this reason, it still speaks to the people of today.

Biography

1571   Born, probably in Milan, on September 29th. His father is a caretaker or architect for Francesco Sforza, Count of Caravaggio, where the family often resides.

1584   Moves to Milan. Serves apprenticeship at the workshop of the Late Mannerist painter, Simone Peterzano

1590   Death of Caravaggio's mother. Moves to Venice.

1592   Moves to Rome. Caravaggio lives in temporary housing; as he falls ill, he is taken in by the Ospedale della Consolazione.

1595   C. lives at the residence of Cardinal Del Monte, his protector, and paints various paintings with religious and artistic subjects.

1599   First official commission for the Contarelli Chapel in San Luigi dei Francesi with the story of Saint Matthew.

1600   Portraits of Saints Peter and Paul for the Cerasi Chapel in Santa Maria del Popolo.

1601   C. lives at the residence of Cardinal Girolamo Mattei. He executes various paintings, among which include *Supper at Emmaus* (now in London).

1603   Sued for defamation of the painter Giovanni Baglione.

1604   Various arrests for possession of unauthorized weapons and assault.

1605   Inflicts injury upon the notary Pasqualone and escapes to Genoa to Prince Doria, where *Ecce Homo* is painted.

1606   *Madonna and Child With Saint Anne* is removed from Saint Peter's Church. Caravaggio kills his rival Ranuccio Tomassoni, flees to the estate of the Colonna family on the outskirts of Rome and paints *Supper at Emmaus* (now in Milan).

1607   Sojourn in Naples (*Madonna of the Rosary* and *Flagellation*).

1608   Stays in Malta, where Caravaggio is inducted into the Knights of Malta on July 14th. He paints the *Beheading of John the Baptist*. After a conflict with another knight, he is imprisoned. He flees to Syracuse and is expelled from the Order.

1609   His flight continues through Messina and Palermo to Naples, where the Knights of Malta pursue, ambush, and injure him.

1610   Anticipating an early pardon from Pope Paul V, C. makes his way towards Rome. On July 18th, he goes ashore to Porto Ercole, falls ill, and dies in a local hospital. He is buried in a mass grave.

Bibliography

The literature on Caravaggio is vast and is continuously expanding. For that reason, only a few easily accessible texts are cited.

–   A. von Schneider, Caravaggio und die Niederländer, Amsterdam 1967.
–   A. Pérez Sánchez, Caravaggio y el naturalismo español, Madrid 1973.
–   M. Marini, Caravaggio e il naturalismo internazionale, Turin 1981.
–   R. Longhi, Caravaggio, Rome 1982.
–   D. Mahon, The singing 'Lute- player'..., London 1990.
–   M. Cinotti, Caravaggio, Bergamo 1991.
–   D. Ponnau, Caravage, une lecture, Paris 1993.
–   B. Berenson, Caravaggio, Milan 1994.
–   M. Gregori, Caravaggio, Milan 1994.
–   C. Strinati/R. Vodret, Caravaggio e i suoi..., Naples 1999.
–   M. Dal Bello, Caravaggio, percorsi di arte e cinema, Cantalupa (Turin) 2007.
–   R. Papa, Caravaggio, Florence 2009.
–   S. Ebert-Schifferer, Caravaggio: Sehen – Staunen – Glauben; der Maler und sein Werk, Munich 2009.
–   S. Schütze, Caravaggio: das vollständige Werk, Cologne 2009.
–   C. Strinati (ed.), Caravaggio, Ausst.-Kat. Scuderie del Quirinale (Rom), Mailand 2010.